The Fami... DISCIPLESHIP BIBLE

NEW TESTAMENT

CHRIS CHAVEZ

Illustrated by
MIKE BROWN

LUCIDBOOKS

WYDEN
PUBLISHING

The Family Discipleship Bible: New Testament

Published by Lucid Books in Houston, TX
www.LucidBooksPublishing.com
and
Wyden Publishing in Katy, TX
www.wydenpublishing.com

ISBN-10: 1-63296-278-0 | ISBN-13: 978-1-63296-278-2 (paperback)
eISBN-10: 1-63296-280-2 | eISBN-13: 978-1-63296-280-5

Special Sales: Most Lucid Books titles are available in special quantity discounts. Custom imprinting or excerpting can also be done to fit special needs. Contact Lucid Books at Info@LucidBooks Publishing.com.

To Heather Chavez—Thank you for who you are. I love you so much, but in putting this book together, I appreciate you in a way I never dreamed. As a helpmate, you are not just some helper who stands by your man, but you are absolutely necessary for me to do anything meaningful in the Kingdom. There is no Chavez family kingdom vision without you. I never knew what I needed, and even today I do not know how much of a blessing you will be to me in the years to come. You stand as the tangible evidence of God's great love for me on a daily basis. I love you and wish I could live out that love much better than I do. Hang in there because God will help me grow into the man you deserve.

To Antonio, Moriah, Samuel, and Thaddeus—This book was driven by my desire to give you as firm a foundation as possible. I can't change your heart, but I can teach you and point you to the good Father who loves you more than I ever will. One day, you will understand that I deeply desired to give you all that I never had. Daddy loves you!

To Dr. Freddie Gage (1933–2014)—Many people evangelize, but an evangelist is someone altogether different. Soul winning is what they breathe. Dr. Freddie Gage taught me more about evangelism just by being who God made him to be than any book or Bible lesson. Words cannot express how grateful I am to have known him. Beyond seeing the evangelistic gift at work, he showed me that loving people means doing what others won't do in order to love people.

Chris Chavez

I want to thank my father, Lt. Col. Gene E. Brown, who passed away during the production of this book. I also want to thank my mother, Regina Brown, whose strong will kept my father alive long enough to ensure his grandkids will always remember their "Pockets." To my loving wife, Cheree, and my four amazing children—Abby, Luke, Lydia, and Phoebe—God has graced me with the most loving family I certainly don't deserve. The patience they have shown me over these past two years discussing the day's events while I was chained to my drawing table has been a true blessing. Last, I would also like to thank Kristin Bergh. Working with you on the colors is always a joy, and I know the difficulty you had working through the loss of your sister.

Michael Brown

Table of Contents

• •

Getting Started with Family Discipleship

Family Discipleship Bible Stories

Family Discipleship Bible Sound Off (Catechism)

Family Discipleship Tools

In Conclusion

Getting Started
with Family
Discipleship

Welcome, Parents!

· ·

We are so glad you've chosen to use this Bible. *The Family Discipleship Bible* was created to equip you as you follow God's command to teach your children the ways of the Lord. In Deuteronomy 6:4–7, we find the clearest call for parents to be the primary teachers in their children's lives.

> Hear, O Israel: The Lord our God, the Lord is one. You shall love the Lord your God with all your heart and with all your soul and with all your might. And these words that I command you today shall be on your heart. You shall teach them diligently to your children, and shall talk of them when you sit in your house, and when you walk by the way, and when you lie down, and when you rise.

Routine devotionals, whether daily or weekly, are only one aspect of discipleship. As you know, children are learning even when we are not intentionally teaching a specific lesson. So parents living out their beliefs are just as important as what they teach, and in most cases, it can be the biggest evangel to children. We truly believe that to be better parents, we must be transformed into the image of Christ more and more.

In the meantime, we hope this resource will help you plant seeds, water, and cultivate the soil of your children's hearts in the hope that God gives the increase (1 Cor. 3:6). Using this resource will strengthen your family relationships and provide an opportunity for you to take the lead in being the primary teacher in your children's lives.

Remember, you are no longer under the law but under God's grace, so having regular devotionals does not earn you anything. That also means that not having regular devotionals does not make you less of a believer, and missing one or two does not bring you shame. There is no condemnation to those in Christ Jesus (Rom. 8:1), so please embark on this parenting journey as a free man who chooses to live as a slave to Christ.

Realize that the path to greater joy is found in fulfilling God's commands. Parents have the incredible opportunity to be part of God's story in the salvation of their children. God needs no one to bring about the salvation of a child, and no one can hinder God from saving a child either. But as we follow God's command of preaching the gospel and making disciples, we find our greatest joy.

Let us as parents embrace our built-in mission field: the home. There, we have the opportunity to freely proclaim the gospel daily in both word and deed. Once a child is saved, we have the built-in opportunity to disciple that child on a daily basis. This Bible is not *the* tool to help you, but it is *a* tool that we hope you find useful. Feel completely free to disagree with some theological concepts as you read the Bible stories and other texts.

Outside of the gospel, there is much freedom in the non-essentials, so if you do not like the wording in a particular story, by all means change it on the fly. The same goes for the catechism. If you find another answer more true to scripture or more in line with what you hope to teach your children about God, please do so. This is not a Baptist, Catholic, Bible church, or Methodist devotional tool but rather a tool any parent can use who would like a little help pointing their child to the most high God. May you find joy in shepherding your family toward God in all things.

Blessings to your family,
Chris Chavez
Author

Devotional Ideas and Templates

What does a family devotional look like?

To be honest, what a family devotional looks like really depends on you. You can use these tools together or mix and match them as you see fit. For instance, if you feel your current devotionals are doing what you hoped they would do but want to start catechizing a bit, you might add a Bible Sound Off element. If that is the case, the catechisms will give you questions to ask your children daily, weekly, or even periodically. A great thing about catechizing is that in many cases, the parents learn the answers as well. So even new believers can disciple their children while they learn too.

The possibilities of what you can do together are endless. You can experiment and see what works best for your family. The good thing about devotionals is that they can evolve as your family grows in size and in the knowledge of God. This Bible is not intended to be a how-to manual but a resource for parents to maximize discipleship in the home.

What it will look like in your home is only limited by your imagination. We hope you sing, act out Bible stories, ask deep questions, and grow just as much as your children.

There are a few samples of how to creatively impart Bible stories on the next page.

Full Devotionals

1. **Toddler Age: Daily or Weekly Devotional before Bed (20–30 minutes)**

   * Read Bible Story (5–10 minutes)
     * The Jesus Storybook Bible is excellent for toddlers
     * Ask simple questions and dialogue about the story
   * Bible Sound Off (5 minutes)
   * Sing Together (5 minutes)
   * Listen (1 minute)
   * Family Prayer (5 minutes)
     * Family, friends, the lost, government leaders
   * Scripture Blessing (2 minutes)

2. **Elementary Age: Daily or Weekly Devotional before Bed (25–40 minutes)**

   * Read Bible Story (5–10 minutes)
     * Ask questions and dialogue about the story
   * Bible Sound Off (5 minutes)
   * Scripture Memorization (5 minutes)
   * Sing Together (5–10 minutes)
   * Family Prayer (5–10 minutes)
     * Family, friends, the lost, government leaders
     * Listen occasionally*
   * Scripture Blessing (2 minutes)

3. Mixed Ages: Daily or Weekly Devotional before Bed (30–45 minutes)

❖ Read Bible Story (10–15 minutes)
  ◇ Act out a story
❖ Bible Sound Off (10 minutes)
❖ Scripture Memorization (5 minutes)
❖ Family Prayer (5–10 minutes)
  ◇ Family, friends, the lost, government leaders
❖ Scripture Blessing (2 minutes)
❖ Parent sings song over each child as final good night
  ◇ Rock smaller children when possible

4. Mixed Ages: Daily or Weekly Devotional before Bed (25–40 minutes)

❖ Read Bible Story (10–15 minutes)
  ◇ Answer questions and dialogue about the story
  ◇ Let them lead the dialogue
❖ Sing Together (10–15 minutes)
❖ Family Prayer (5–10 minutes)
  ◇ Family, friends, the lost, government leaders
  ◇ Listen occasionally*
❖ Scripture Blessing (2 minutes)

Partial Devotionals (Late Nights, Driving Home, Hectic Day)

1. Toddler Age: (10–15 minutes)

❖ Parents Read Story from Jesus Story Book Bible (5 minutes)
  ◇ Highlight important themes, ideas

❖ Family Prayer (5 minutes)
◇ Family, friends, the lost, government leaders

❖ Father's Blessing (2 minutes)

2. Mixed Ages: (10–15 minutes)

❖ Parents Read Bible Story from Any Children's Bible
◇ Highlight important themes, ideas

❖ Family Prayer (5 minutes)
◇ Family, friends, the lost, government leaders

❖ Father's Blessing (2 minutes)

3. Mixed Ages: (10–15 minutes)

❖ Bible Sound Off (5 minutes)

❖ Family Prayer (5 minutes)
◇ Family, friends, the lost, government leaders

❖ Father's Blessing (2 minutes)

4. Mixed Ages: (15–25 minutes)

❖ Read Bible Story (5–10 minutes)
◇ Highlight key ideas

❖ Family Prayer (5–10 minutes)
◇ Family, friends, the lost, government leaders

❖ Father's Blessings (2 minutes)

Other Simple Devotional Ideas

1. Act out a Bible story with homemade costumes.
2. Teach children your favorite worship songs.
3. Pick out a country, learn about it, and pray for that country.
4. Walk around the block and pray for your neighbors.
5. Celebrate the anniversary of God answering a family prayer. For example, God saved Grandma from cancer last year. Lesson: Remembering past victories gives us hope in future struggles.
6. Form a circle and place pictures of a missionary family in the center. Then pray for them by name.

Listen – One thing parents forget to do is just listen to God. We would all agree that both our flesh and the enemy speak lies to us—*You're not smart. You can't do it. You're ugly. You're a bad kid*—and other lies. We can dismiss them as harmless or we can be intentional about teaching our kids how to "take every thought captive" (2 Cor. 10:5).

A simple practice is to have your children listen to God. Give them a simple question to repeat and then help them match it with God's character so they can learn to recognize truth. We want to teach them to battle lies like Jesus did—with the truth found in scripture—but first we need to help them recognize lies. Here's an example: "How do you feel about me, God?" If they "hear" something, you can ask if that sounds like something God would say. You should always preface your questions with the fact that whether or not they hear something is not the point and certainly doesn't make them better than anyone else. The point is to remember that God wants to talk with us, and we should honor Him by just "listening" from time to time. Having them listen helps them learn to practically understand that God loves to build up and not tear down. And it is always important to ask if they remembered a scripture during prayer. It highlights the fact that God's predominate way of speaking to us is through His word.

Tools Provided in This Book

. . . .

27 Bible Stories with Questions and Answers Provided

After reading a story, it's useful to have prepared questions with answers so any parent can feel confident that they are drawing out key elements of the story. The questions and answers are intended to help teach the children, help them develop a more robust view of the story, and provide a solid foundation for understanding all the scriptures.

Bible Sound Off/Catechism (Three Provided)

To catechize means to instruct systematically, especially with questions, answers, explanations, and corrections. Therefore, a catechism is the manual or questions used to catechize someone. In order to avoid any negative connotations with the word *catechism*, we have chosen to simply call this tool Bible Sound Off. From early church history to the present day, this time-tested tool helps teach biblical truths that are vital for a good understanding of who God is and what His word says.

At first glance, it might seem that catechizing small children won't work, but it's amazing how much toddlers can absorb. In fact, the early years of development is when a parent wants to input as many facts as possible. As children develop, these facts become the well from which they draw when their brains develop reasoning.

Even with children as young as two or three, you can do one question per week and cover 52 questions in a year. You will be amazed at how they remember the answers and even more amazed at how you remember them. The best thing is that since you are the one reading the questions with the answers in front of you, you don't need to know anything. Many parents, including the author, have ended up catechizing themselves as they catechize their children.

You can research this more online. *Family Shepherds: Calling and Equipping Men to Lead Their Homes* by Voddie Baucham Jr. will show you how this could fit into family discipleship.

Scripture Blessings

These blessings are simply scriptures that have been somewhat personalized so a father, mother, grandparents, or even older siblings can pray them over children. This simple nightly ritual not only gives fathers and mothers the ability to pray scripture over their children, but it also creates the anticipation of being blessed by a parent each night. The common method is for the father or mother to place his or her hand on the head of each child and speak these blessings. In addition, these prayers can be used to teach a child to bless others such as siblings or even parents. You can have a different child pick the blessing each night and enjoy the look in their eyes as they try to find the perfect one. Children Desiring God has produced a tool called *A Father's Guide to Blessing His Children* that you can purchase to gain a Biblical understanding of a blessing. In fact, many of the blessings we provide are inspired by this resource, and some of them are the same. All credit to them for letting us ride on their coattails.

Song Recommendations

Children shouldn't be the only ones to sing to God and about God. They need to see their parents praise Him as well. The songs recommended are not any more foundational than other songs. But our hope is that your family will discover songs that become your family songs and that your children would see mom and dad model praising God in the home. A great idea is to find videos of these songs on the Internet so they can learn the melody.

Dictionary of Common Biblical Terms

These are very brief definitions that hopefully remain true to the Bible but are easy to understand.

Brief Summary of Old Testament Books for Reference or Memorization

These are simple, concise summaries that will give you quick insight into each book. As children get older, they might become good memory tools for knowing the Bible better.

Memory Passage Suggestions for Memorization

One thing I lament is that I was only taught single verses as a child. But childhood is the best time to learn chunks of scripture. Children's brains are not developed enough to reason and fully think through a devotional, but they can retain large amounts of information. Childhood is the best time to input as much as possible so as they age, they can grow from memorizing to working with the information and then to reasoning. Memorizing at an early age ensures that they have a deep well from which to draw.

Some tips: Use hand motions for each verse when possible. It makes it fun and also aids in memory. For instance, for "The Lord is my shepherd; I shall not want" (Ps. 23:1), simply point to the sky when you say *Lord* and point to yourself when you say *my*. It really is that simple. My kids have been learning Romans 8 for a while now, and we have motions for some of the verses and not for others. It isn't about having the perfect hand motions for each verse. It is about filling their minds with Bible passages that will be embedded in their hearts and minds. Just do what works for your family whether it's hand motions or memorizing each verse to a rhythm—anything that aids in memory.

Family Discipleship Bible Stories

1

Announcement of John the Baptist

(Luke 1)

God planned everything before He created anything. God the Father, God the Son, and God the Holy Spirit waited for just the right time to reveal what they planned: a "good" creation including Adam who was "very good." But Adam's sin broke the goodness God created and opened the door for death to come to all people. Then years later, God revealed that through a man named Abraham, one nation would be special, and all the families of the earth would be blessed through him. But just like God told Abraham, his descendants were enslaved in a foreign land. God was silent for 400 years before raising someone—Moses—to deliver them from Egyptian slavery.

In a similar way, God was silent for 400 years before raising up the deliverer of all deliverers. God's chosen people, Israel, were in the land God promised Abraham, but because of their disobedience, they were still being ruled by foreign nations. The Romans ruled much of the world, including all of the promised land. Then, like a much-needed breath of fresh air, God sent an angel named Gabriel with a special message. Gabriel appeared to a priest named Zechariah while he was burning incense before the Lord in the temple. Zechariah and his wife, Elizabeth, were righteous people, but she was still unable to have a child. Gabriel told him that his prayers had been answered and that his wife Elizabeth would have a son. This was a wonderful message, but it still gripped Zechariah with fear.

Gabriel said that the child would have a special job that would change everything. They were to name him John, for he would prepare the way for the anointed one, the Messiah, and he would be filled with the Holy Spirit even before birth.. Even after Gabriel told him all this, Zechariah questioned how he could know it truly would happen. Gabriel said, "You will be silent and unable to speak until the day that these things take place, because you did not believe my words" (Luke 1:20). The people wondered why Zechariah had been in the temple so long. When he came out, unable to speak, they understood that he must have seen a vision.

Now when the time came for Elizabeth to have her baby, it was a son, just like Gabriel said. And when it was time to name him, Elizabeth said they were going to name him John. Everyone questioned her because they assumed he would be named after someone from their family, and John was not a name in their family. They immediately turned to Zechariah to find out what he thought the child's name should be. He asked for a tablet and wrote "His name is John" (Luke 1:63), and immediately he could speak again. It brought great awe to everyone there, and all who heard wondered how special the child would be.

~~~~~~~~~~~~~~~~~~~~ **Questions:** ~~~~~~~~~~~~~~~~~~~~

❝ What caused Zechariah to lose his speech?

   ✧ *Zechariah didn't believe Gabriel.*

❝ What was going to be special about John?

   ✧ *He would prepare the way for the anointed one, the Messiah.*

❝ How was John special even before he was born?

   ✧ *He was filled with the Holy Spirit.*

Bible Stories

2

Announcement of Jesus to Mary

(Luke 1; Matthew 1)

With John the Baptist, the forerunner of the Messiah, on the way, the next step in God's plan was to announce His Son. Once again, God sent the angel Gabriel with a message. This time, Gabriel went to Nazareth in Galilee and said to a young virgin named Mary, "Greetings, O favored one, the Lord is with you!" (Luke 1:28). Naturally, Mary was startled, but Gabriel told her not to be afraid because she had found favor with God. "And behold, you will conceive in your womb and bear a son, and you shall call his name Jesus. He will be great and will be called the Son of the Most High. And the Lord God will give him the throne of his father David, and he will reign over the house of Jacob forever, and of his kingdom there will be no end" (Luke 1:31–33).

Mary asked how this could be since she was a virgin. The angel answered, "The Holy Spirit will come upon you, and the power of the Most High will overshadow you; therefore the child to be born will be called holy—the Son of God" (Luke 1:35). Unlike Zechariah, Mary answered in belief: "Behold, I am the servant of the Lord; let it be to me according to your word" (Luke 1:38). Mary rejoiced in song over what God was going to do through her.

But Mary was engaged to a man named Joseph, so having a child that was not his was quite a problem. Once again, God sent an angel, this time to Joseph, and told him to keep his marriage plans with Mary. The angel spoke to Joseph in a dream that the baby in Mary's womb was conceived by the Holy Spirit. When he awoke, Joseph did exactly as he was told in the dream. Months later, just as God said, Mary gave birth to a son—Jesus.

With that, God's plan to come down from heaven and save His chosen people had begun. Jesus—all of God poured into skin, the deliverer that not only Israel had been waiting for but the deliverer the Gentiles didn't even know they needed—was coming.

Questions:

66 How did the angel tell Mary she would conceive since she was a virgin?

◇ *The Holy Spirit would come upon her, and the power of the Most High would overshadow her.*

66 How did the angel appear to Joseph?

◇ *The angel appeared to Joseph in a dream.*

66 Did Mary do anything to be selected as the mother of Jesus?

◇ *No, Mary didn't do anything. She was chosen because she found favor with God.*

Bible Stories

3

Birth of Jesus

(Luke 2)

After Joseph and Mary were married, Caesar Augustus, the ruler of Rome, decreed that everyone must return to their hometown to be counted. That meant that because they were descendants of King David, they would have to leave Nazareth and travel to Bethlehem. But by the time they made it to Bethlehem, Mary was ready to give birth. However, there was no place for them to stay. So with no place to stay, Mary gave birth to Jesus, wrapped him in swaddling clothes, and laid him in a manger. How could this be? Isn't this the Messiah that was announced by an angel? How could God not gather all the important people of the city to witness his birth?

Right after Jesus was born, God did gather some people, but not the people we would think. Out in the fields, in the dark of night, some shepherds were watching their flock. With the glory of the Lord shining around him, an angel appeared to them. Naturally, they were filled with fear, but the angel said, "Fear not, for behold, I bring you good news of great joy that will be for all the people. For unto you is born this day in the city of David a Savior, who is Christ the Lord" (Luke 2:10–11).

And as if that wasn't enough, right after telling the shepherds where to find Jesus, a multitude of angels filled the sky praising God. The angels could have been sent to anyone, but God chose to tell shepherds. So when the angels left, the shepherds went and found Jesus right where they were told. They shared with Joseph and Mary all the angels had told them. As you can imagine a mother would do, Mary treasured every word in her heart. After seeing God's salvation, the shepherds returned to their flock, praising God for all they had seen and heard.

As always, God's ways are not man's ways. The birth of Jesus certainly gives us insight into how different God's plan is than what Israel was expecting.

Questions:

❝ Why did Mary and Joseph have to leave Nazareth and go to Bethlehem?
  ◇ *Because they were both descendants of King David.*

❝ Who did the angel tell the shepherds was born in Bethlehem?
  ◇ *A savior who is Christ the Lord*

❝ Joseph and Mary were both descendants of what person?
  ◇ *King David*

4

Baptism of Jesus

(John 1; Matthew 3)

In those days, John the Baptist was preaching a message of repentance in all Judea. As prophesied in the book of Isaiah, John, a forerunner to the Messiah, was preparing the way. He wore clothing made of camel's hair and a belt of leather. His food was locusts and honey. His simple lifestyle was matched by his simple message: "Repent, for the Kingdom of God is at hand" (Matt. 3:2). And throughout Judea and Jerusalem, people were coming out to be baptized by him in the Jordan River. But when the Pharisees and Sadducees came to him, he called them a brood of vipers and told them to bear fruit in keeping with repentance. It didn't matter if they claimed Abraham as their father because "God is able from these stones to raise up children for Abraham" (Matt. 3:9).

When John saw Jesus, he said, "Behold the Lamb of God, who takes away the sin of the world! This is he of whom I said, 'After me comes a man who ranks before me, because he was before me.' I myself did not know him, but for this purpose I came baptizing with water, that he might be revealed to Israel" (John 1:29–31). Jesus came to John and asked him to baptize him.

Even though John didn't think he should baptize Jesus, when Jesus told him that it needed to be done to fulfill all righteousness, John chose obedience and agreed.

As Jesus was baptized and came up from the water, the heavens opened, and the Spirit of God descended like a dove and rested on him. Then a voice from heaven said, "This is my beloved Son, with whom I am well pleased" (Matt. 3:17).

And with that, the good news that God was taking back the world he created began.

Questions:

❝ Why was Jesus baptized?
  ◇ *To fulfill all righteousness.*

❝ Why do you think John spoke to the Pharisees and Sadducees the way he did?
  ◇ *Because being a physical descendant of Abraham does not entitle you to salvation.*

❝ Why do you think John called Jesus the Lamb of God?
  ◇ *Because just like Israel sacrificed lambs to atone for sin, Jesus would sacrifice himself like a sacrificial lamb.*

5

Temptation of Jesus

(Matthew 4; Luke 4)

After the Spirit descended upon Jesus when he was baptized, the Spirit led Him on a path that none of us would imagine. The Spirit led him into the desert where Jesus fasted for 40 days and 40 nights. After all that time without food, as you can imagine, Jesus was hungry. He was right where the Spirit wanted him to be. Now is when He was to be tempted by Satan, also called the devil, which means slanderer or accuser.

Right away the devil said, "If you are the Son of God, command these stones to become loaves of bread" (Matt. 4:3). But Jesus quickly answered by quoting from the book of Deuteronomy: "Man shall not live by bread alone, but by every word that comes from the mouth of God" (Matt. 4:4).

Once more, the devil tried to tempt Jesus by taking Him to the very top of the temple. There he challenged Jesus to throw Himself down. The devil tried quoting from the book of Psalms where it says God would send angels to make sure Jesus would not be harmed. But Jesus knew he was not using God's words correctly. So quoting Deuteronomy again, He said, "You shall not put the Lord your God to the test" (Matt. 4:7).

Finally, the accuser took Jesus to a very high mountain and showed Him all the kingdoms of the world. He told Jesus that he could give these kingdoms to whomever he wanted, and he would give them to Jesus if He would only fall down and worship him. But Jesus quickly said, "Be gone, Satan! For it is written, 'You shall worship the Lord your God and him only shall you serve'" (Matt. 4:10). It's interesting that Jesus quoted from Deuteronomy again, but instead of calling him the accuser, He called him Satan, which means adversary.

And with Jesus's command to be gone, the devil left Him. Then God sent His angels to minister to Jesus, and when He returned to Galilee, He returned in the power of the Spirit.

Questions:

❝ What did Jesus do every time He was tempted, and what does that teach us?
  ✧ *He quoted God's word, and we should know the Bible to battle just like Jesus.*

❝ What book of the Bible did Jesus quote from?
  ✧ *The book of Deuteronomy*

❝ What do the names devil and Satan mean?
  ✧ *Devil means slanderer, and Satan means accuser.*

❝ Who do you think gave the devil the kingdoms and why?
  ✧ *God, because somehow it is all part of His plan.*

6

Jesus at the Wedding Feast

(Matthew 4; John 2)

With the power of the Spirit resting on Him, Jesus began to minister to the Jewish people in power. He went throughout Galilee preaching the good news of the kingdom, healing every disease and every affliction. As His fame spread, people brought their friends who were sick, demonized, or suffering from physical disabilities. Jesus healed them all.

As He traveled, preaching the kingdom and healing the sick, Jesus gathered 12 disciples. These were not important men. They were not teachers or leaders or even scholars. In fact, they were mainly just fishermen, and even a tax collector. Their names were Simon (called Peter) and his brother Andrew, James and John (sons of Zebedee), Philip and Bartholomew, Thomas and Matthew, James, Thaddaeus, Simon the Zealot, and Judas Iscariot (who would eventually betray Him).

Jesus's miracles were signs to let everyone know that God sent Him. His first miracle took place at a wedding. The celebration looked like it would have to end because they ran out of wine. Mary, Jesus's mother, was there, and when she found out, she ran and told Jesus. But Jesus asked what that had to do with Him because His time had not yet come. But in great faith that Jesus would extend the celebration, Mary told his disciples to do whatever He asked.

Now there were huge jars that each held about 30 gallons of water. Jesus gave instructions to fill them with as much water as each could possibly hold. When all of them were full, He told them to draw some water and take it to the master of the wedding celebration. Even though they knew that it was only water, they trusted Jesus and took it to the master of the banquet. But when the master tasted the water, it became wine, and not just wine, but the best wine he had ever tasted. It was so good that the master went to the groom and said that people always give good wine in the beginning but switch to a poor wine once people drank a lot. But not this time. This time, the best wine was saved until last.

Questions:

66 How many disciples did Jesus have?

⬦ *Twelve.*

66 Where did Jesus perform his first miracle?

⬦ *At a wedding celebration.*

66 What was Jesus's first miracle?

⬦ *He turned about 30 gallons of water into the best wine so the celebration could continue.*

7

Jesus's Power over Demons

(Mark 5)

One of the most wonderful things about Jesus is the comfort He gives. His power extends not only to the things we can see, but also to the things we cannot see. Jesus has power over the angels that followed Satan, now called demons. These demons are always trying to cause problems for people so they will not trust God. But never ever ever do they stop Jesus from loving his people.

One day after Jesus crossed the Sea of Galilee, a man met Him who had an unclean spirit, or demon. The man was so tormented that he lived among the tombs. Things had gotten so bad that when people tried to bind him with chains, he would just break them. There was no one who could match his strength. But when Jesus stepped off the boat, the man saw Jesus from afar, ran to him, and fell down before Him.

Crying out in a loud voice through the man, the demons said, "What have you to do with me, Jesus, Son of the Most High God? I adjure you by God, do not torment me" (Mark 5:7). Jesus asked, "What is your name?" and he said his name was Legion because "we are many" (Mark 5:9). They begged Jesus not to send them out of the country but instead to send them to a herd of pigs nearby. Jesus allowed them to flee to the pigs, and immediately after they went to them, the herd rushed down into the water and drowned.

When people heard about this, they came to see what had happened. What they found was the man who was once tormented dressed in clothes and in his right mind. Those who had seen it were scared and begged Jesus to leave. As Jesus got in a boat to leave, the man begged to go with Him. But Jesus told him to go home to his friends and tell them how much God had done for him and the great mercy he had experienced.

Questions:

66 Who did the demons recognize Jesus as?

✧ *The Son of the Most High God*

66 Were the demons more powerful than Jesus?

✧ *No. In fact, they begged him not to torment them.*

66 What did Jesus tell the man who had been delivered from the demons?

✧ *To go tell his friends what God did for him and the great mercy he experienced.*

66 Who has power over the things we can see and the things we cannot see?

✧ *Jesus*

8

Parable of the Sower

(Matthew 13) (A parable is a made-up story that tells a spiritual truth.)

Because of all the mighty things Jesus said and did, great crowds came to see and hear Him. Stepping in a boat and pushing out just a little bit from the shore was one of his ways to make sure everyone could hear the wonderful things He had to say. It was while sitting in a boat and speaking to a great crowd that He told one of His most famous parables—the parable of the sower. A sower is someone who sows or plants seed in hopes of gathering a great harvest when the seeds grow.

Jesus told of a sower who spread some seeds, and as he did, they landed in different places. Some seeds landed on the road and were quickly eaten by the birds. Other seeds fell on the rocky soil and quickly started to grow. But because the soil wasn't deep enough, the roots could not grow deep, and the plant withered in the hot sun. Some of the seeds fell among the thorns and weeds. When these seeds tried to grow, the weeds choked them out. But there were some seeds that landed right where the sower wanted them to land, right on good, rich, fertile soil. The seeds that landed there produced a harvest, some a hundredfold, some sixtyfold, and some thirtyfold. Jesus ended his story with these words: "He who has ears, let him hear" (Matt. 13:9).

Jesus's disciples asked what the parable meant and why Jesus used parables. Jesus told them He used parables because the prophet Isaiah's words must be fulfilled, that most of the Jews would have ears but not hear. This had to do with their years of disobedience that hardened their hearts and left them resistant to hear what God had to say. Jesus went on to tell them how blessed they were because God never leaves his people without hope. God gave them eyes that see and ears that hear.

Jesus then explained the parable. The seeds are the words of the kingdom, and the different soils represent the hearts of those that hear the words. The seed sown along the road represents those who might hear the words with their ears but don't understand them. Then the evil one comes and snatches away what was sown in their hearts. As for the seeds sown on the rocky ground, these are people who hear the word proclaimed, and it seems like they receive it with great joy. But when times get tough or they are treated badly, they quickly turn away from God because they have no roots. The seed sown among the thorns represents the people who hear the word proclaimed, but their love for riches and for the things of the world choke the words that were sown, and they don't bear fruit. But the seed sown on the good soil represents those who hear, understand, and obey the word. They bear fruit, some a hundredfold, some sixtyfold, and others thirtyfold.

~~~ **Questions:** ~~~

❝ Why did Jesus tell parables?

◇ *To fulfill the prophecy of Isaiah that many Jews would hear but not really understand because of their hardened hearts.*

❝ Does the seed need to land on good soil to produce fruit, or can it land anywhere?

◇ *The seed needs to land on good soil.*

❝ Should you just assume your heart is good soil, or should you ask God to make your heart good soil?

◇ *I should always pray that God makes my heart good soil so I can hear, understand, and obey.*

9

The Good Samaritan

(Luke 10) (A parable is a made-up story that tells a spiritual truth.)

One of the most powerful parables Jesus told was in response to a question by a lawyer. At that time, a lawyer was an expert in the law of Moses. The lawyer was trying to test Jesus and asked what he needed to do to inherit eternal life. Jesus answered his question with another question: "What is written in the Law? How do you read it?" (Luke 10:26). The lawyer answered that you should love God with all your heart, soul, strength, and mind and love you neighbor as yourself. Jesus told him that was a great answer and that if he lives like that, he would have eternal life. But the lawyer's deep pride stirred up one more question that he asked Jesus: "And who is my neighbor?" (Luke 10:29). Jesus answered with a parable.

He told the story of a man traveling from a faraway land when suddenly robbers attacked him. They beat him, took everything he had, and left him for dead on the side of the road. As he lay there, a priest came down the road. When the priest saw the man, he crossed the road and passed by on the other side. Then a Levite came along and did the same thing. He crossed to the other side of the road. But then a Samaritan, people whom the Jews hated, came along and saw the man. The Samaritan had compassion on him.

He went to him, took care of his wounds, set him on his own donkey, and took him to an inn to recover from the beating. The Samaritan left the next day. But before he left, he gave some money to the innkeeper and said, "Take care of him, and whatever more you spend, I will repay you when I come back" (Luke 10:35).

Jesus then asked the lawyer which of the men proved to be a neighbor to the man who was robbed and beaten. The lawyer quietly answered, "The one who showed him mercy." Jesus simply said, "You go, and do likewise" (Luke 10:37).

Questions:

❝ What two characters in the story refused to stop and help the man who was robbed and beaten?

  ◇ *The priest and the Levite*

❝ What character did stop and help the man who was robbed and beaten?

  ◇ *The Samaritan*

❝ Who is your neighbor?

  ◇ *Anyone with a need that God brings in your path.*

10

The Prodigal Son

(Luke 15) (A parable is a made-up story that tells a spiritual truth.)

Jesus told another parable that went like this. There once was a man who had two sons. The sons gladly lived with their father until the time came to start their own families. But the man's younger son could not wait to do what he wanted to do. The problem was that he didn't have any money, so he told his father that he wanted his inheritance now. An inheritance is what a father gave to his son, who would receive it after the father died. Asking for his inheritance now revealed how selfish the son was. Not only did he want what he would get if his father were dead, but he also wanted to leave his family to go do what he wanted to do.

With a heavy heart, the father divided his property and gave the younger son his share of the inheritance. Just like that, the son was off to do the things his heart felt like doing. He traveled to faraway lands chasing fun and recklessly spending money. He spent the last of his money at the worst possible time. There was a severe famine in the land, and he needed food. The son found work in that faraway land feeding a man's pigs. Finally, at his lowest point, as he found himself wishing he could eat the pig food, he suddenly remembered how good his father's servants lived. So he decided to go home.

On the way home, he practiced his speech: "Father, I have sinned against heaven and before you. I am no longer worthy to be called your son. Treat me as one of your hired servants" (Luke 15:18–19). But the son had no idea that his father had been waiting and hoping for him to come home.

And when the day came that the son was far off, the father saw him and started running. Filled with compassion, he ran to him and joyously hugged him and kissed him. Confused, all the son could think to do was say the words he had been practicing all the way home. Not listening to his son's pleas, the father called his servants saying, "Bring quickly the best robe, and put it on him, and put a ring on his hand, and shoes on his feet. And bring the fattened calf and kill it, and let us eat and celebrate. For this my son was dead, and is alive again; he was lost, and is found." (Luke 15:22–24).

When the older son saw and heard all the commotion over the return of his brother, he refused to join in the celebration. In disgust, he told his father that he had never done anything like the younger brother, and yet he never even received a small goat to celebrate. The father simply said, "Son, you are always with me, and all that is mine is yours. It was fitting to celebrate and be glad, for this your brother was dead, and is alive; he was lost, and is found" (Luke 15:31–32).

Questions:

66 Had the father forgotten all about his younger son, or had he been hoping and looking for him to return?
  ◇ *The father was looking and hoping for his son's return.*

66 Did the father accept him back as a servant or joyfully give him all the benefits of being his son?
  ◇ *The father joyfully received him back as his son.*

66 Do you think the older brother was prideful about how good he was, or do you think he was grateful for having a loving father with great wealth?
  ◇ *The son was prideful about his good behavior.*

11

Jesus Raises Lazarus from the Dead

(John 11)

There are many stories in the Bible that show us that God doesn't always do things the way we think He should. One of those stories is about a man named Lazarus who lived in Bethany with his sisters, Mary and Martha. The sisters were kind and loving friends of Jesus, and Lazarus was also greatly loved by Jesus. So when Lazarus became sick, the sisters sent word to Jesus, hoping He would come quickly to heal him. But when Jesus heard the news, He chose to stay in the city where He was for another two days.

After those two days had passed, Jesus told His disciples it was time to go to Bethany. He said, "Our friend Lazarus has fallen asleep, but I go to awaken him" (John 11:11). Jesus's disciples thought He was talking about Lazarus sleeping because he was sick, but Jesus quickly corrected them. He plainly said that Lazarus had died.

By the time Jesus made it to Bethany, Lazarus had been buried in the tomb for four days. When Martha heard that Jesus was coming, she ran out to meet Him and said that if He had been there, she knew that Lazarus would still be alive. Jesus told her that Lazarus would rise again. Knowing Jesus would not lie to her, Martha believed Him. Jesus said, "I am the resurrection and the life. Whoever believes in me, though he die, yet shall he live, and everyone who lives and believes in me shall never die. Do you believe this?" Martha said, "Yes, Lord; I believe that you are the Christ, the Son of God" (John 11:25–27).

As Jesus came to the place where Lazarus was buried, Mary and some of the Jews who were mourning met Him. With tears filling her eyes, Mary said the same thing, that if He had been there, she knew Lazarus would still be alive. It was then that Jesus began to weep. Some of the Jews noticed that and realized how much Jesus loved Lazarus. They also wondered that if Jesus could heal a blind man, why couldn't he save Lazarus? Jesus gave the command for the stone to be rolled away from the entrance to the tomb. Martha warned him that because it had been four days, there would be a very bad smell. Jesus said, "Did I not tell you that if you believed you would see the glory of God?" (John 11:40). As they took away the stone, Jesus lifted His eyes toward heaven and prayed aloud so that all could hear. He thanked the Father that He already heard Him because He knew the people needed to hear Him pray so that they would believe the Father sent him. As He finished His prayer, Jesus cried, "Lazarus, come out" (John 11:43). And just like that, Lazarus rose up and came out of the tomb. He was still bound by the linen burial cloths that covered his body. Jesus said, "Unbind him, and let him go" (John 11:44). After seeing this miracle, many believed in Jesus.

Questions:

❝ When Jesus heard about Lazarus, did he go immediately or did he stay where He was?

◇ *Jesus stayed where He was for two more days.*

❝ What did Jesus say about those who believed in Him?

◇ *Those who live and believe in Him would not die.*

❝ Why did Jesus pray aloud?

◇ *So when He raised Lazarus, the people would believe that the Father sent Him.*

12

Jesus Heals a Centurion's Servant

(Luke 7; Matthew 8)

The Jews have always been God's special people. Jesus made it clear that He was sent here for the lost sheep of Israel. But Jesus came to be a light to the Gentiles as well. One day, after His most famous sermon that we call the Sermon on the Mount, Jesus made his way to Capernaum. It was there that Jesus met a Gentile man who had great faith.

A Roman centurion had a servant who was so sick that he was about to die. The centurion valued the man and was willing to do anything he could to save him. When the Roman centurion heard that Jesus was entering the city, he used his influence to reach out to Jesus. He asked the Jewish elders to ask Jesus to come and heal his servant. So the elders asked Jesus to help this Gentile. They told Jesus how much the centurion had done for the Jewish people and how he even spent his own money to help build a place for them to worship God. Hearing this, Jesus decided to go to the centurion's home. As Jesus neared the house, the centurion met him.

What the centurion said next amazed Jesus. "Lord, I am not worthy to have you come under my roof, but only say the word and my servant will be healed. For I too am a man under authority, with soldiers under me. And I say to one, 'Go,' and he goes, and to another, 'Come,' and he comes, and to my servant, 'Do this,' and he does it" (Matt. 8:8–9). Hearing this, Jesus told the crowd that followed Him that He had not found that kind of faith in all of Israel.

Jesus went on to say that many would come from the east and west and would celebrate with Abraham, Isaac, and Jacob, while many Jews would be cast out where there is weeping and gnashing of teeth. By this, Jesus was saying that through faith, Gentiles from all over would enjoy the kingdom of God. Jesus told the centurion to go home, and that because he believed, his servant was healed. And his servant was healed in that moment, just like Jesus said.

Questions:

66 Was Jesus's primary ministry on earth to the Jews or the Gentiles?
  ◇ *It was to the Jews.*

66 What did the centurion recognize that the Jews did not?
  ◇ *That Jesus had the authority from God to heal.*

66 What does it take to be part of God's kingdom?
  ◇ *The faith to believe in Jesus.*

Bible Stories

13

Jesus Heals Blind Bartimaeus

(Mark 10)

Crowds began to follow Jesus everywhere He went so they could hear the things He said and see the things He did. One day, Jesus and His disciples were traveling to Jericho. They came upon a blind man sitting on the roadside begging. His name was Bartimaeus. When Bartimaeus heard that it was Jesus of Nazareth, he began to cry out for Jesus to have mercy on him. Although he was blind, Bartimaeus believed something about Jesus that others couldn't see with their natural eyes. Bartimaeus called Jesus the Son of David, which meant he believed that Jesus must be the descendant of King David who would be the Messiah. Hearing this, Jesus stopped and told his disciples to call him over.

The people could hear Bartimaeus crying out to Jesus. But instead of having compassion on him, they told him to be quiet. They didn't believe that a blind beggar could be important to Jesus. But that did not stop Bartimaeus. In fact, instead of being quiet, he yelled even louder. Jesus then asked the sweetest question a blind beggar could hear: "What do you want me to do for you?" (Mark 10:51). Blind Bartimaeus didn't ask for anything other than what he wanted most: his sight.

Jesus is the very definition of compassion—seeing someone in need, caring, and then acting to help that person in some way. Jesus, the compassionate Messiah, said, "Go your way; your faith has made you well" (Mark 10:52). And immediately Bartimaeus could see, and he began to follow Jesus.

Questions:

❝ Did Bartimaeus display faith in Jesus even before asking for sight?

◇ *Yes, when he called him "Son of David," he showed that he had faith that Jesus was the Messiah.*

❝ What does it mean to be compassionate?

◇ *To see, care, and act when someone is in need.*

❝ Jesus told Bartimaeus that what made him well?

◇ *He said his faith had made him well.*

14

Jesus Walks on Water

(Matthew 14; Mark 6)

Jesus did many great miracles. These were signs that He was the Messiah, God's chosen one. On a couple of occasions, He fed 5,000 people with only a handful of fish and bread. After one of those amazing days where thousands of hungry people listened to him teach all day and then were miraculously fed, Jesus told the disciples to get on a boat and go to the other side of the lake while he dismissed the crowds. After the crowds left, Jesus did his favorite thing and went up on the mountain to pray. Time passed by quickly while he was alone with God, and by evening, his disciples' boat was a long away from land.

Unlike Jesus who was in the peaceful presence of the Father, the disciples were in a terrible storm all night. The wind and the waves were crashing against their small fishing boat. Around 4:00 a.m., when things seemed the darkest, Jesus came to them, walking on the water. As you can imagine, when they saw Him, they were immediately terrified. In fear they cried, "It is a ghost!" (Matt. 14:26). With great compassion, Jesus immediately spoke to them saying, "Take heart, I am. Do not be afraid" (Matt. 14:27)*.

* See original Greek text.

Hearing this, the disciple Peter said, "Lord, if it is you, command me to come to you on the water." Jesus simply said, "Come" (Matt. 14:28, 29). So Peter got out of the boat and began walking on the water, just like Jesus. But when Peter felt the wind, fear replaced his faith, and he began to sink. "Lord, save me," Peter cried out (Matt. 14:30). Jesus immediately took hold of his hand. As he lifted him up, Jesus said, "O you of little faith, why did you doubt?" (Matt. 14:31).

After a long night of battling a storm, being frightened by a ghost only to find out it was Jesus, watching Peter get out of the boat and walk on the waves, seeing Peter begin to sink, hearing him cry out to Jesus, and then watching Jesus easily rescue him, the disciples must have been ready for this storm to end. Amazingly, as soon as Jesus got into the boat, the wind and waves stopped. The disciples began to worship Jesus, saying, "Truly you are the Son of God" (Matt. 14:33).

Questions:

❝ After miraculously feeding 5,000 people, what did Jesus do?

⋄ *He went alone to the mountain to pray.*

❝ Jesus said, "Take heart; it is I. Do not be afraid" when the disciples were scared (Matt. 14:27). What did he mean by saying *I am*?

⋄ *By saying I am, Jesus was saying he was God.*

❝ Peter followed Jesus's command and walked on water, too. What caused him to begin to sink?

⋄ *His fear replaced his faith.*

15

Jesus at Passover

(John 13; Matthew 26)

One of the most spectacular times in Jerusalem was the celebration of the Feast of Passover. Three times a year, Israel—God's chosen people—were to come to Jerusalem. This particular feast was for the people of Israel to remember how, on the night before God delivered them out of Egypt, an unblemished lamb was sacrificed, and its unblemished blood was placed on their doorposts. That night, God sent His final plague on Egypt. The Angel of Death killed the firstborn of every household but "passed over" the homes of the Jewish people who covered their doorposts with the blood of a spotless sacrificial lamb.

On this particular Passover, Jesus knew that His work on earth was done and that it was time to return to the Father. Jesus had the disciples prepare a room where they could celebrate together. Now, the devil had already put it into the heart of Judas Iscariot to betray Jesus. Judas agreed to lead the Jewish soldiers to Jesus for 30 pieces of silver.

During the meal, Jesus got up from the table, took off His outer garments, and did something only servants do. He took a basin of water and began to wash the feet of all 12 of his disciples—not just 11 of them, but Judas Iscariot as well. He knew that just like the sacrificial lamb was slaughtered to save Israel from death,

He was going to be killed very soon. Jesus knew He would be arrested, tried, and killed even though He was blameless. This final act before returning to the Father was His final lesson to his disciples. After He washed their feet, He explained to them that a servant is not greater than the master. He showed them that to be great, you must be a servant.

Then Jesus took some of the unleavened bread and gave it to them. Breaking and blessing the bread, He said, "Take, eat; this is my body" (Matt. 26:26). Then He took the a cup of wine and gave it to them saying, "Drink of it, all of you, for this is my blood of the covenant, which is poured out for many for the forgiveness of sins" (Matt. 26:27–28). Despite all this, the disciples still didn't fully understand everything that was about to happen. After they finished, Jesus and His disciples sang a hymn and then left.

Questions:

❝ How did Jesus teach and show greatness?
 ✧ *By washing the feet of His disciples, even the feet of Judas Iscariot.*

❝ What feast did Jesus celebrate with His disciples before he was arrested?
 ✧ *The Passover*

❝ What did Jesus call the bread and the wine He gave His disciples?
 ✧ *His body and blood.*

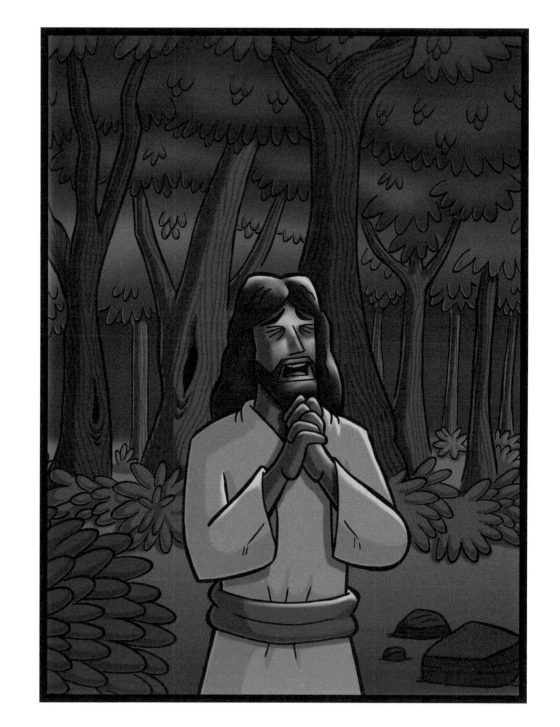

16

Jesus Betrayed in the Garden

(Matthew 26; Luke 22)

After Jesus and His disciples celebrated Passover, He took them to a place called the garden of Gethsemane. Gethsemane was an oil press located on a slope of the Mount of Olives. It was a place Jesus often went to pray. Jesus told Peter, James, and John how extremely sorrowful He was in His soul and for them to stay awake and pray. He then went by Himself and did what He loved best—talk with His Father. Falling on His face, Jesus poured out His soul in prayer. Knowing what He was about to endure, Jesus asked if there was any other way, if it was possible for this cup to pass from Him. But as He cried out in anguish, He also rested in hope and said, "Nevertheless, not as I will, but as you will" (Matt. 26:39).

After praying for a while, Jesus went to check on Peter, James, and John. Instead of finding them in prayer, He found them asleep. He woke Peter up and asked him why he couldn't even stay awake an hour. Even with a sorrowful heart, Jesus still took the time to remind Peter of the way to overcome temptation. "The spirit indeed is willing, but the flesh is weak" were His words as Jesus left again to pray (Matt. 26:41). And again, Jesus prayed and asked if there was another way. But again, He submitted to the Father's will above His own. Taking a second break, He found His disciples asleep again. So for a third time, Jesus went to pray by Himself, praying the same prayer.

Returning to His disciples after praying for the third time, He woke them and told them He was about to be betrayed into the hand of sinners. While He was still speaking, Judas Iscariot, one of the 12 disciples, came with a great crowd armed with swords and clubs. The crowd had been sent by the chief priests. Judas had agreed to betray Jesus in exchange for 30 pieces of silver. Walking right up to Jesus, Judas used the sign he gave the chief priests so they would know which one was Jesus. Judas gave Jesus a kiss. Jesus said, "Friend, do what you came to do" (Matt. 26:50).

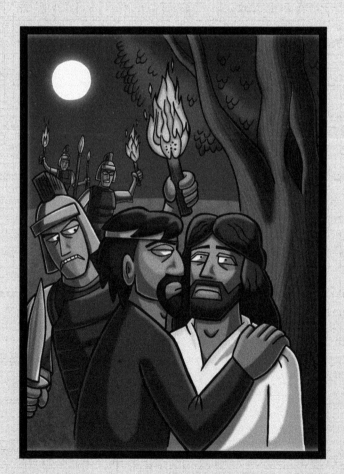

As the soldiers took Jesus, Peter lashed out in anger with his sword and cut off the ear of one of the chief priests' servants. Jesus told Peter to put away his sword and then said, "Do you think that I cannot appeal to my Father, and he will at once send me more than twelve legions of angels? But how then should the Scriptures be fulfilled, that it must be so?" (Matt. 26:53–54). Jesus then took the servant's ear and miraculously reattached it, completely healed, good as new. And as they arrested Jesus and led Him away, the disciples fled.

～ **Questions:** ～

❝ Did Jesus know what was about to happen, and if so, what did He do before?

✦ *Yes, Jesus knew what was about to happen, so He prayed.*

❝ How did Jesus conclude each of His prayers?

✦ *"Not as I will, but as you will" (Matt. 26:39).*

❝ Could Jesus have stopped His arrest, and if so, why didn't He?

✦ *Yes, He could have easily, but He didn't so that scripture could be fulfilled.*

17

Jesus Falsely Accused, Persecuted, and Condemned to Death

(Matthew 26, 27; Luke 23; Mark 14)

The night Jesus was arrested, He endured three trials in addition to an incredible amount of humiliation and persecution. He was first taken before the high priest, Caiaphas, where there were other scribes and elders gathered together. They gathered witnesses that were supposed to lie so they could condemn Jesus to death. The problem was that even the witnesses could not get their testimonies to agree.

Through all the accusations, Jesus remained quiet until the high priest said, "I adjure you by the living God, tell us if you are the Christ [Messiah], the Son of God." Jesus answered, "You have said so. But I tell you, from now on you will see the Son of Man seated at the right hand of Power and coming on the clouds of heaven" (Matt. 26:63–64). Hearing this, the high priest tore his robe, and all the leaders agreed that Jesus should be put to death. At this point, some began to spit on Him. Then others covered His eyes, hit Him, and mocked Him by asking, "Who is it that struck you?" (Matt. 26:68).

As morning came, the chief priests decided that by sending Jesus to Pilate who governed Jerusalem for Rome, they could have Him put to death. So they brought

Jesus to Pilate. For his own reasons, Pilate did not want to get involved, so when he heard that Jesus was from Galilee, he sent him to King Herod. Herod was a ruthless king appointed by Rome to rule the Jews in a large part of Rome, including Galilee. Herod had heard stories of Jesus for a while and was eager to finally talk to Him. But after questioning Jesus and getting no answers, he and his soldiers mocked Jesus, dressed Him in kingly clothes, and sent Him back to Pilate.

When Jesus came before Pilate again, Pilate gathered all the Jewish leaders and told them he found that Jesus was not guilty of any of the charges against Him. Pilate said that even Herod didn't find anything wrong. So Pilate told them, "Look, nothing deserving death has been done by him. I will therefore punish him and release him" (Luke 23:15–16). So the soldiers scourged Jesus and even mocked Him by placing a crown of thorns and a purple robe on Him. Pilate wanted to release Jesus and thought the beating would satisfy the Jewish leaders, but the leaders and people all shouted "Crucify, crucify him!" (Luke 23:21). Fearing a riot

and what that might do to his position with Rome, Pilate saw he had nothing to gain by releasing Jesus. So while the crowd was watching, Pilate washed his hands and said, "I am innocent of this man's blood; see to it yourselves" (Matt. 27:24). Jesus was the stripped of his clothes and turned over for crucifixion.

~ Questions: ~

❝ Did the Jewish leaders try to find the truth about Jesus or create lies about Him?
   ◇ *They created lies about Him so they could condemn Him.*

❝ Did the Roman governor Pilate or King Herod find any fault in Jesus?
   ◇ *Neither found Him guilty of anything.*

❝ Did Pilate accept responsibility for Jesus's crucifixion?
   ◇ *No, by washing his hands before the crowd, Pilate declared he was innocent of His blood.*

18

Crucifixion of Jesus

(Mark 15, 27; Luke 23; John 19)

Roman crucifixion wasn't just about putting someone to death. It was meant to publicly torture the person to death. This is the type of death that Pilate turned Jesus over to. John the Baptist's words—"the Lamb of God, who takes away the sin of the world" (John 1:29)—came to life as Jesus traveled to a place called Golgotha. When Jesus got there, already bloody and bruised from the scourging, the soldiers gambled to see who could keep His clothes. Then they nailed Jesus to a wooden cross and placed it between two thieves.

Even as Jesus hung there in terrible pain, the Jewish leaders made fun of him, saying, "Are you not the Christ [Messiah]? Save yourself and us!" (Luke 23:39). And even one

of the thieves crucified alongside Jesus railed at Him by mockingly telling Him to save Himself since He is the Messiah. But the other thief said, "Jesus, remember me when you come into your kingdom" (Luke 23:42). Having endured all the torture up to that point, Jesus somehow replied to him, "Today you will be with me in paradise" (Luke 23:43).

Around noon that day, darkness came over the land until about 3:00 p.m. It was then that Jesus cried out, "Father, into your hands I commit my spirit!" (Luke 23:46). With the final words, "It is finished," He yielded up His spirit (John 19:30). At that very moment, the temple veil, which separated God's presence from the rest of the temple, was ripped from top to bottom, forever changing things for Jews and Gentiles. When God tore the veil, He symbolically opened His presence up to all people. The tearing of the veil was so powerful that the earth shook, tombs were opened, and many saints were raised from the dead. Even a soldier who felt and saw the earth shake was filled with awe and said, "Truly this was the Son of God!" (Matt. 27:54).

When evening came, a respected member of the council, Joseph of Arimathea, took Jesus's body from the cross. Jesus's body was then wrapped in cloth strips and laid in a tomb that had been cut out of a rock. When the body was secured in the tomb, a large stone was rolled in front of the entrance. But the next day, the Pharisees were so worried about Jesus's body being stolen and people claiming Jesus had risen from the dead that they had Pilate seal the tomb and place soldiers there to guard Jesus's body.

Questions:

66 Was Roman crucifixion meant to just kill people or to torture them and send a message for all to see?
  ◇ *It was meant to torture and send a message to all.*

66 How did the thief, who is getting what his actions deserve and can't do anything to make up for them, still get to go to paradise?
  ◇ *By believing that Jesus was the Son of God.*

66 Why is it such a big deal that the temple veil was torn in two?
  ◇ *Because God was no longer going to separate His presence from His people.*

19

Resurrection

(Mark 16; Matthew 28; John 20; Luke 24)

Early in the morning, three days after Jesus died, a few women, including Mary Magdalene, went to the tomb to anoint Jesus's body. But when they arrived, even though it was still dark, they could see that the stone had been rolled away. When they went inside the tomb, an even bigger surprise was waiting. They did not find Jesus's body. Instead, two angels dressed in spectacular white robes were there. As you can imagine, the women were scared, but one of the angels said, "Do not be afraid, for I know that you seek Jesus who was crucified. He is not here, for he has risen, as he said" (Matt. 28:5–6). Then the angels told the women to go tell the disciples that Jesus would meet them in Galilee.

So with both great fear and great joy filling their hearts, the women ran to tell the disciples. But before they reached the disciples, Jesus met them, and they fell to His feet and worshiped him. Once again, Jesus told them not to fear but to tell the disciples to meet Him in Galilee. When the women finally found Peter and John to tell them all that had happened, the disciples could not believe it. Peter and John both ran to the tomb and saw that not only was Jesus's body gone, but the linens that covered his body were left there, neatly folded.

Some of the soldiers who had been ordered to guard the tomb went and told the chief priests all that happened. But sadly, instead of believing Jesus was the Messiah and telling all the Jewish people in Jerusalem, the chief priests paid the soldiers to tell people that Jesus's disciples came by night and stole His body. So the soldiers took the money and spread the lie.

The first couple of men to see Jesus didn't even know it was Him. As they were walking to the village called Emmaus, they talked about all that had happened the last few days. While they were walking, Jesus approached them and asked what they were talking about, but because their eyes were not opened, they did not know it was Jesus. Immediately they questioned where He had been, because everyone knew about all the uproar Jesus had caused in Jerusalem. So they told of all the mighty works Jesus had done and how they hoped He was the Messiah they had been waiting for. But then they told how He was condemned and crucified.

Jesus replied, "O foolish ones, and slow of heart to believe all that the prophets have spoken!" (Luke 24:25). And then beginning with Moses, Jesus properly interpreted the scriptures concerning Himself. When they finally got to Emmaus, Jesus sat at the table with them, broke bread, and blessed it and gave it to them. Immediately their eyes were opened, and just as quickly, Jesus disappeared.

Questions:

66 How did the women know that Jesus rose from the dead and His body was not just stolen?

 ⬦ *Because angels told them, and then Jesus appeared to them.*

66 What did the chief priest do to try to hide the truth?

 ⬦ *They paid the soldiers to tell lies.*

66 What does Jesus point the men walking to Emmaus to in order to show them about Himself?

 ⬦ *He pointed them to everything recorded in the scriptures that had to do with Him.*

Bible Stories

20

Great Commission and Ascension

(Luke 24; John 20; Matthew 28; Acts 1)

The evening following the conversation Jesus had with the men walking to Emmaus, while the disciples were gathered together in fear of the Jewish leaders, Jesus came and stood among them and said, "Peace be with you" (John 20:19). As you can imagine, the disciples were scared, thinking it was a spirit of some kind. Jesus told them not to doubt but to touch His hands and feet so they would know it was really Him. Yet still, even with Jesus alive and standing in front of them, it was extremely difficult to understand that this was really happening. So Jesus pointed them to the scriptures and opened their minds to fully understand what they could not see before. Now they realized that the Messiah must suffer, die, and then rise from the dead on the third day. They understood that repentance and forgiveness of sins would be proclaimed to all nations, beginning in Jerusalem.

Over the next 40 days, Jesus appeared to more than 500 people. But soon, it was time for Jesus to return to the Father, and He needed to give His final directions to the disciples. He had them gather on the Mount of Olives, and there He spoke all the words they would need. He said, "All authority in heaven and on earth has been given to me. Go therefore and make disciples of all nations, baptizing them in the name of the Father and of the Son and of the Holy Spirit, teaching them to observe all that I have commanded you" (Matt. 28:18–20). Then He told them to wait in Jerusalem until they were clothed in power from on high. He told them that soon they would be baptized with the Holy Spirit.

The disciples asked Jesus if this was the time He would restore the kingdom to Israel. But it was not their place to know God's timing. Instead, Jesus said, "But you will receive power when the Holy Spirit has some upon you, and you will be my witnesses in Jerusalem and in all Judea and Samaria, and to the end of the earth" (Acts 1:8). And with those final words, He ascended into the clouds out of their sight. With the disciples still looking to the heavens and with His final words fresh in their minds, two angels appeared in white robes. They told the disciples that just as Jesus had ascended, one day He would return in the same way. And with that, the disciples returned to Jerusalem filled with joy.

~ **Questions:** ~

❝ What did Jesus point His disciples to in order to understand all the events of His life, death, and resurrection?

◇ *He showed them the scriptures.*

❝ The soldiers lied that Jesus's body was stolen. How many people did Jesus appear to after rising from the dead?

◇ *More than 500 people.*

❝ Jesus gave them what we call the Great Commission, but what was needed first?

◇ *They needed to be clothed with power from on high.*

Bible Stories

21

Pentecost and the Holy Spirit

(Acts 2)

Long ago when Moses came down from Mt. Sinai with the ten commandments and Israel agreed to keep the Torah (law), God created a special feast. The Jews called it Shavuot (or Pentecost). You might even call it a wedding day in a way because that is the day God gave Himself to Israel and Israel gave themselves to God. The day was 50 days after God powerfully freed Israel from slavery in Egypt. Now once again, 50 days after Jesus, the eternal Son of God, was raised from the dead, God was about to do something even more incredible than give Himself through the Torah. As He prophesied in the Bible books of Joel and Jeremiah, one day He would pour his Spirit on all flesh and write His law on their hearts.

So the disciples were in Jerusalem, gathered in an upper room 50 days after the resurrection of Jesus. "And suddenly there came from heaven a sound like a mighty rushing wind, and it filled the entire house where they were sitting. And divided tongues as of fire appeared to them and rested on each one of them. And they were all filled with the Holy Spirit and began to speak in other tongues as the Spirit gave them utterance" (Acts 2:2–4). Because the city of Jerusalem was such a center of activity, there were men from every nation there. The sound and commotion created by the Spirit being poured out drew many together to see what

97

was happening. Surprisingly, each person heard the disciples speaking in their own language, which led them to ask, "What does this mean?" (Acts 2:12).

Peter, now filled with the Spirit of God for the first time, finally understood and was able to explain to everyone what this meant. He explained that they were not drunk with wine or crazy, but instead, God was pouring out his Spirit. Peter told them how they had wrongly persecuted Jesus to the point of crucifying Him on a cross but how God raised Him from the dead. And not only was He raised from the dead, but He was the Messiah (Christ) they had been longing and waiting for. With God's Spirit so active and powerful, the people cried out, "What shall we do?" (Acts 2:37). Peter joyfully told them to believe in Jesus as Messiah and, be baptized, and they too would receive the gift of the Holy Spirit.

The lives of 3,000 people were changed that day when this good news filled their hearts. The good news that trusting in Jesus was the way of salvation was the mystery hidden away in God's promise to Abraham. The promise that all the families of the earth would be blessed through Him was completed in Jesus. Now this good news, or gospel, was about to spread to the ends of the earth, just like Jesus said it would.

~~~~ Questions: ~~~~

❝ What did God give to his disciples 50 days after Jesus's resurrection?
✧ *He gave the gift of the Holy Spirit.*

❝ Who makes it possible for people to understand the good news?
✧ *God the Holy Spirit.*

❝ What is the news called that reveals Jesus is the way of salvation?
✧ *The good news, or the gospel.*

22

Ordinary Man, Extraordinary Power

(Acts 6, 7)

After Pentecost and the giving of the Spirit to believers, more and more people believed as the gospel spread day by day. With more disciples, there was more prayer and teaching that needed to be done, so much, in fact, that other needs such as making sure the widows were taken care of began to distract Jesus's disciples. By this time, people began calling the disciples apostles, which means "sent ones." The apostles didn't want to neglect the widows, but they also knew they couldn't do it all by themselves. So they gathered all the believers together and told them they needed to focus on prayer and the ministry of the word. They said they needed them to pick out seven men full of the Spirit, well thought of by others, and wise in all they did. One of the seven men chosen was a man named Stephen. He was full of faith and the Holy Spirit, so much so that even though Stephen wasn't one of the 12 disciples, he was doing great signs and miracles among the people. It was clear that it wasn't a name or title that made one powerful but rather faith and being full of the Spirit.

Little by little, leaders who opposed the gospel tried to send in people to argue with Stephen. But anyone they sent could not stand up to his Spirit-empowered wisdom. Since that didn't work, they tried telling lies about him, knowing that if they could convince people he was speaking against Moses and God, everyone would turn from listening to him. Their plan worked, and the elders and scribes dragged Stephen before the council. False witnesses told how Stephen spoke against the Torah and that he was saying that Jesus came to change all the things Moses taught. But even with all the lies being said about him, everyone could see the power that rested on him because his face had the peace and power of an angel.

Standing before the council, Stephen started with Abraham and traced, step-by-step, the history of Israel, including how Israel rebelled against God. But it was his final words that absolutely enraged the people. Stephen called them stiff-necked people who always resist the Holy Spirit, and, just like their forefathers, persecuted the prophets. He said they persecuted and killed Jesus who was the Messiah (Christ). As he finished, he cast his gaze upward and said, "Behold, I see the heavens opened, and the Son of Man standing at the right hand of God" (Acts 7:56).

With those words still hanging in the air, the people grew enraged. They seized Stephen, dragged him out of the city, and stoned him to death. A man named Saul of Tarsus was there, and the witnesses laid their cloaks at his feet before they stoned Stephen. But even with stones being hurled at Stephen from every direction, he still cried out for God to forgive them. And with those last few words, the stones took the life from Stephen, and he became the first martyr.

~ **Questions:** ~

❝ What did people call the disciples, and what does it mean?

◇ *They called them apostles, which means sent ones.*

❝ How could Stephen do mighty signs and miracles?

◇ *He was full of faith and the Spirit.*

❝ What was the name of the man watching with approval as Stephen was stoned?

◇ *Saul of Tarsus*

23

Saul Becomes Paul

(Acts 8–9)

The day Stephen was stoned marked the beginning of a great persecution in Jerusalem. Even though many people believed Jesus was the Messiah (Christ), there were still many Jews who did not. Thinking that they were defending God, they attacked Jesus's followers with great anger. Saul of Tarsus, who approved of the killing of Stephen, even started going from house to house to imprison anyone who believed in Jesus. But even as the believers were scattered, they kept proclaiming the good news as they went, doing the very thing Jesus said they would do, starting in Jerusalem and moving to Judea, then Samaria, and eventually to the ends of the earth. Persecution did not stop the good news; it only helped spread it.

But Saul's murderous anger kept him chasing down disciples wherever he could find them. And with the approval of the high priest, Saul traveled to Damascus to drag more disciples back to Jerusalem to be punished and imprisoned. As Saul traveled, a bright light from heaven shown down, and he fell to the ground. He heard a voice say, "Saul, Saul why are you persecuting me?" (Acts 9:4). It was Jesus's voice, the very one Saul was persecuting. Jesus not only spoke to him, but he also blinded him. The men traveling with Saul had to guide him the rest of the way to Damascus.

Now Ananias was a disciple in Damascus who had heard of Saul's violent persecution. Jesus came to him in a vision and told him to go find Saul, but Ananias didn't want to. Jesus told him "Go, for he is a chosen instrument of mine to carry my name before the Gentiles and kings and the children of Israel. For I will show him how much he must suffer for the sake of my name" (Acts 9:15–16). Hearing this, Ananias went and found Saul, just like he was told. Saul was still blind and tired because he had not eaten in three days. But God told him in a vision that a man named Ananias would come and lay his hands on him so he could regain his sight. As Ananias prayed for Saul, scales fell from Saul's eyes. He regained his sight and was filled with the Holy Spirit.

Filled with the Holy Spirit, Saul became a new person that no one could recognize. No longer was he known as Saul from Tarsus but as Paul, an apostle of Jesus the Messiah (Christ). Paul was well trained in the Torah (law) and was now empowered with the Spirit of God. He not only taught other Jews about Jesus, but he was uniquely called to reach the Gentiles, too.

Questions:

66 What caused the good news to spread?

◇ *The persecution of the church.*

66 What happened to Saul on his way to Damascus?

◇ *A bright light surrounded him, and he fell to the ground. Jesus spoke to him and blinded him.*

66 What happened when Ananias prayed for Saul?

◇ *Scales fell from Saul's eyes, his sight returned, and he was filled with the Holy Spirit.*

24

The Holy Spirit Comes to Gentiles

(Acts 10; Deuteronomy 7)

Because God planned everything from the beginning, He was using something bad—the persecution of Christians—to do His good work. You see, God is the one who chose Abraham, and God is the one who chose his son Isaac, and God is the one who chose to make Isaac's second son Jacob into a nation. He changed Jacob's name to Israel, and his descendants became the nation of Israel. God didn't choose Egyptians, Philistines, Jebusites, or any other Gentile nation to be His special people—only Israel. And it wasn't because they were the best but just because it made God happy. Out of His great mercy, God always had a plan to reach people from every nation. In fact, in God's promise to Abraham, He told him that he would be a blessing to all nations. Israel had been the only nation with special access to God, but now everything was changing. No longer would Gentiles be on the outside longing to be inside.

Peter had become the leader of the disciples. He was at a friend's house praying when God gave him a vision. In this vision, Peter saw something like a sheet with all kinds of animals on it. But the animals were the types of animals that Israelites, according to the Torah, were not allowed to eat. So when Peter heard the words, "Rise, Peter; kill and eat," he immediately refused because he loved to obey the Torah given by God (Acts 10:13). Peter heard this message three times, and each time, God added, "What God has made clean, do not call common" (Acts 10:15). Of course, that confused Peter, and he didn't know what it meant.

What Peter did not know was that days earlier, God came in a vision to a Gentile named Cornelius. Even though Cornelius was a Gentile, he feared God and loved others just like God would want. In the vision, God told Cornelius to send some men to Peter and bring him back. The men Cornelius sent arrived just as Peter was trying to understand the vision. God quickly spoke to Peter, telling him to go with the men because he had sent them. That confused Peter even more because Jews stayed away from Gentiles as much as possible, so to go to one of their houses just didn't make sense. But Peter did not question God, and he went with the men the next day.

When Peter arrived, Cornelius fell at Peter's feet and worshiped him, but Peter quickly told him to stop because he was only a man. Cornelius told Peter about his vision. Then Peter understood that God's purpose was to use Jesus's sacrifice to clean people other than Jews. So when Cornelius asked Peter to tell him what God said, Peter said, "Truly I understand that God shows no partiality, but in every nation anyone who fears him and does what is right is acceptable to him. . . . And he commanded us to preach to the people and to testify that he is the one appointed by God to be judge of the living and the dead. To him all the prophets bear witness that everyone who believes in him receives forgiveness of sins through his name" (Acts 10:34–35, 42–43).

And when Peter finished his sentence, the Holy Spirit fell on the Gentiles just like on the Jews at Pentecost. God had opened Peter's eyes to understand that it was always His plan to be the God of the people from every nation. For many years, Gentiles had been far from God, but now, because of Jesus's sacrifice, the Spirit of God made them clean and empowered them just like the Jews. So the first Gentile Christians were baptized, and Peter went and told the rest of the disciples what had happened. Now they, too, understood God's plan and glorified Him.

Questions:

66 Before this story, did Gentiles have access to God like the Jewish people?
   ◇ *No, God only chose the nation of Israel as His special people.*

66 Was the giving of the Holy Spirit to Gentiles a new plan or something God had already planned?
   ◇ *It was always God's plan to give the Gentiles the Holy Spirit.*

66 Before, God dwelled in the inner part of the temple. Where does his Spirit dwell now?
   ◇ *The Spirit now dwells in believers, who are now His temple.*

25

Becoming Who You Are

(New Testament Epistles)

Like the other apostles, Paul was used mightily to spread the good news to Jews, but he was also given a special job to reach the Gentiles. Spreading the good news also meant that God's kingdom was overtaking the evil one's kingdom, and that brought great opposition. Many Jews would not believe Jesus is the Messiah (Christ), and many Gentiles hated the changes that came about when new believers turned from idols. But God can't be stopped, and He used Paul to keep preaching and teaching. He gave Paul great understanding, and as more and more people believed, many questions arose. So Paul wrote letters to help them understand.

To the people of Rome he wrote his most complex letter that explains how God justifies, or makes righteous, both Jews and Gentiles.

To the people of Corinth, he wrote two letters. In the first one, he corrects their mistakes and answers their questions. And in the second letter, he confirms their faith, defends his apostleship, and warns them of false teachers.

To the people of Galatia, he explains how returning to the Torah (law) for justification is actually running from the freedom found in God's grace.

To the people of Ephesus, he encouraged believers to live fruitful lives in the power of God's grace.

To the people of Philippi, Paul taught of the joy found in Messiah (Christ).

To the people of Colossae, Paul proclaimed Messiah's (Christ's) sovereignty over all and taught that believers are now alive in Christ.

To the people of Thessalonica, he wrote two letters. In the first letter, he exhorted believers to continue in faith and eagerly await the Messiah's (Christ's) coming. In the second letter, he reminded them to stand firm in their faith and correct the misunderstanding that Messiah (Christ) had already returned.

To a friend named Timothy he wrote two letters. In the first letter, he encouraged Timothy and gave some leadership guidelines for the believers in Ephesus. In the second letter, Paul reminded Timothy to fight the good fight of faith and be prepared to engage unsound teachings.

To a friend named Titus he laid out the characteristics of those who have spiritual authority in the church and told how older and younger believers should relate to one another.

Paul reminded an old friend Philemon that the slave who ran away from him now follows Jesus, so Philemon should forgive him and accept him as a brother.

As you can see, Paul was entrusted with much to say to the Gentile believers. Over and over, the words God gave him helped grow and strengthen believers everywhere. Some insights were practical for daily living, while other letters were deep views about the tiny details of God's ways. But more than anything, we find that Paul wanted people to become who they already are in Christ. God used and still uses Paul's letters to help us know who we are in Christ. Sanctification is the slow process of God transforming us into the image of Jesus, full of grace and truth. Because we are in Him and empowered by the Spirit, we don't have to do things for God but simply be who we are by giving ourselves over to the Spirit and turning away from our earthly passions. Throughout Paul's 13 letters, we find deep truths that help us be who we already are in Christ.

Questions:

❝ What was the apostle Paul's special job?
  ◇ *He was to reach the Gentiles.*

❝ How many letters did Paul write that are in the Bible?
  ◇ *Thirteen letters.*

❝ What does sanctification mean?
  ◇ *It is the process of God transforming us into the image of Jesus.*

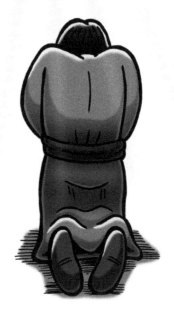

26

Jesus Is Better

(Book of Hebrews)

No one knows for sure who wrote the book of Hebrews, but the book helps everyone understand just how special Jesus is and how everything had always been pointing to Him. The scriptures pointed to a Messiah who would be fully man and fully God, a God-man. Because of this, it is our faith in Him that should guide and strengthen us. The point is that Jesus is better.

For years, God gave the prophets messages to deliver to His people, but finally, God sent the message itself—Jesus. No longer did they have to imagine what God was like because Jesus is the exact imprint of God's nature. Throughout the years, God had angels deliver messages and give directions. Angels are powerful and awe-inspiring, and they were seen as more important than any man. But Jesus was not just any man. He is the Son of God, and that makes Him far better than angels.

Jesus is even greater than Moses. That is what so many needed to hear to encourage them to put all their faith in Jesus. Many of God's people could not imagine anyone greater than Moses. Hebrews teaches that Moses was only a servant in God's house, but Jesus is God's Son, and a son is always greater than a servant. Jesus is better than Moses.

And even the high priest who got to enter the presence of God once a year is not greater. He had to offer a sacrifice for himself because his sins also needed to be covered. But Jesus is an even better high priest. Like us, He was human and suffered. But unlike us, He never sinned. So when He made a sacrifice, He didn't have to offer a sacrifice for Himself but instead made Himself a sacrifice to cover our sins. The sacrifices were made once a year, and when the high priest died, another high priest had to take his place. But Jesus's sacrifice was once and for all, because after He offered it, He sat down at the right hand of God. Jesus is the better high priest.

The Torah appointed high priests in connection with the covenant God made with Israel. But that covenant was only with Israel. Even the temple was only a shadow of the real temple in heaven. The new covenant would not be written on stone like the one given to Moses, but instead, God would write it on the hearts of His children. Even the covenant that Jesus is the high priest of is better than the old one. Jesus is the high priest of a better covenant.

The Jews and Gentiles need to be reminded of these things. Because Jesus is better, we should put our full faith in His finished work. Faith has always been what matters. Abraham, whom God chose to be a blessing to all nations, exercised his faith. So did Abel, Enoch, Noah, Joseph, Moses, Samson, Gideon, and more of the mighty men and women of the Bible who pleased God with their faith. Jesus is the founder and perfecter of our faith. Since God never changes, our continued faith should drive us to love each other and follow God no matter what.

Questions:

66 How is Jesus different than the prophets?

◇ *The prophets delivered God's message, but Jesus is the message.*

66 How is Jesus greater than the angels?

◇ *Jesus is the Son of God.*

66 How did all the heroes of the Bible please God?

◇ *They pleased God with their faith in Him.*

27

Jesus Is Coming Back

(Book of Revelation)

History tells us that most of the disciples were killed because of their faith in Jesus. John, exiled to the island of Patmos, was the last to die. While on Patmos, God sent an angel to give John a revelation. It was given to encourage believers to eagerly await Jesus's return, but it also served as a warning of the judgment that people who don't trust in Jesus would endure. The book is actually a revelation of Jesus, which means the revelation is about how God plans to reveal Jesus to the world. A revelation does not tell of something new but instead reveals what has been hidden. The first time Jesus came, He came as a servant to only a small part of the world. His ministry was short, and his earthly ministry had a specific purpose. But when Jesus comes the second time, He will come to the entire world. For those who don't know Him, they should fear this day of the Lord. For those who believe in Jesus, it will be the fulfillment of their great joy.

The first part of the vision given to John holds messages to send to seven specific churches. The messages speak about how each church in that area was either doing well or doing poorly. But these messages were also sent to speak to us today about how we can overcome the same issues they faced.

In John's vision, Jesus is called "the Lamb slain from the foundation of the world" because God wanted to remind everyone that He planned all of this before He made everything (Rev. 13:8 KJV). There is judgment coming, but not before He fulfills all His promises to His people. There is a mighty deceiver coming in a strong powerful way. This false prophet will do mighty works and lead the masses into further darkness.

During this time, there will be a mighty revival of belief among the Jews. The same nation that despised and rejected their Messiah will someday believe to the point of enduring great persecution because of their love for Him. God, who keeps His promises, made it clear through His prophets that He would fulfill all his promises to Abraham, Isaac, and Jacob. Jesus will return in glory, majesty, might, and power to the whole world. A great battle will take place with Jesus easily slaying the enemy with the sword that comes from His mouth. But even better will be the coming day when the evil one will be defeated and judged once and for all. On that day, God will judge everyone according to what they have done. Then death, the evil one, and all whose names are not written in the book of life will be cast into the lake of fire.

And the revelation of Jesus Christ ends with what we expect from such a wonderful Savior. It ends with hope. There will be a new heaven and a new earth. There will be no more death and no more pain. God will wipe away all tears. There will be no light from lamps or the sun because God will be their light. There is coming a day when all who believe in Jesus, both Jew and Gentile, will freely dwell in God's presence. Finally, God's chosen from among every nation and every tribe will be with their God and they will be His people, forever enjoying and reigning with Him.

Questions:

66 What happened to John on the Island of Patmos?
◇ *He received a revelation of Jesus Christ.*

66 What happens to many Jews in the days ahead?
◇ *Many will believe that Jesus is the Messiah (Christ).*

66 What happens to the evil one and death?
◇ *They are both cast in the lake of fire.*

66 Do people from only one nation worship God and reign with Him forever?
◇ *No, God chose people from among every nation and every tribe.*

Bible
Sound Off
(Catechism)

Introductory (Ages 2–8)

66 **1. Who made you?**
  ⋄ *God*

66 **2. What else did God make?**
  ⋄ *God made all things.*

66 **3. Why did God make all things?**
  ⋄ *For His own glory.*

66 **4. Why do things work as they do?**
  ⋄ *God has so decreed it.*

66 **5. How do we learn about God?**
  ⋄ *God reveals Himself.*

66 **6. Where does God reveal Himself?**
  ⋄ *In His word, nature, dreams, and visions.*

66 **7. What does God reveal in nature?**
  ⋄ *His character, law, and wrath.*

66 **8. What more is revealed in His word?**
  ⋄ *God's mercy toward His people.*

66 **9. Where is God's word found?**
  ⋄ *The Bible is God's word.*

66 **10. How many Gods are there?**
  ⋄ *God is one: God the Father—God the Son—God the Holy Spirit.*

Catechism

11. Where is God?

◇ *He is everywhere.*

12. How long has God existed?

◇ *He has always been.*

13. Who is God?

◇ *God is the first and best of all beings.*

14. What is God like?

◇ *God is a spirit, is eternal, and is a personal being. He is perfect in holiness and is all-powerful and all-knowing.*

15. How does God relate to creation?

◇ *God is the creator, redeemer, preserver, and ruler of the universe.*

16. How is man unique?

◇ *He bears God's image.*

17. Who was the first man?

◇ *Adam*

18. What was Adam like at creation?

◇ *He was good.*

19. Did Adam remain good?

◇ *No, he sinned.*

20. What is sin?

◇ *Any thought or deed that doesn't bring God glory.*

21. What does it mean to give glory?

◇ *To show honor and enjoy God as the greatest.*

❝ 22. What is the penalty for sin?
✧ *Death.*

❝ 23. What did Adam's sin bring?
✧ *Death came to all men.*

❝ 24. How did Adam's sin affect men?
✧ *We all sinned in Adam.*

❝ 25. Must all men die for their sins?
✧ *No, God elected some to life.*

❝ 26. How may we be saved from sin and death?
✧ *Only through faith in Jesus Christ.*

❝ 27. Who is Jesus Christ?
✧ *The eternal Son of God.*

❝ 28. Did Jesus ever sin?
✧ *No, only He is righteous.*

❝ 29. What did Jesus do for His people?
✧ *He conquered sin and death.*

❝ 30. How did He conquer sin and death?
✧ *He absorbed God's wrath for sin by dying, then rose again.*

❝ 31. What else did Christ conquer?
✧ *All his enemies.*

❝ 32. Are His enemies powerful?
✧ *They have come to nothing.*

❝ 33. What did Jesus give to His people?
✧ *His own righteousness.*

66 34. What did Jesus take from His people?

✧ *All their sin.*

66 35. How is Christ's work brought to His people?

✧ *By the Holy Spirit.*

66 36. What does the Holy Spirit do?

✧ *He gives life through faith.*

66 37. What is faith?

✧ *Complete trust in what God says because of who He is.*

66 38. How do we recognize true faith?

✧ *It yields good works.*

66 39. Who are God's children?

✧ *Those who love and trust Jesus.*

66 40. What are all God's children called when they gather?

✧ *His church.*

66 41. What are the traits of His church?

✧ *Love for one another.*

66 42. Who is head of the church?

✧ *Jesus Christ.*

66 43. Is His church perfect?

✧ *No, it is being perfected.*

66 44. When will it be perfect?

✧ *After Christ's return.*

66 45. What happens to the earth when Christ returns?

✧ *God creates a new heaven and earth.*

Catechism

❝ **46. What happens to men when Christ returns?**
 ✧ *Christ judges all men's deeds.*

❝ **47. What happens to those Christ judges?**
 ✧ *The righteous dwell with Him forever, and the guilty perish apart from Him forever.*

❝ **48. What is the bad news for all men?**
 ✧ *All have sinned, and all stand condemned.*

❝ **49. What is the good news?**
 ✧ *In mercy, God made a way to save sinners through Jesus's life, death, and resurrection.*

❝ **50. How do we know we are God's children?**
 ✧ *The Spirit of God bears witness with our spirit that we are children of God.*

❝ **Bonus – What is the good news?**
 ✧ *In mercy, God made a way to save sinners through Jesus's life, death, and resurrection.*

❝ **(Long Version)**
 ✧ *There is one God who made everything seen and unseen. He made man in His image. He made him good, but man sinned. God would be just if He punished man forever for his sin, but in His infinite mercy, God made a way to save man. He sent Jesus, the eternal Son of God, fully God and fully man, to live a life we should have lived. Jesus suffered and died a death we deserved, but by the power of the Spirit, He was raised from the dead. He ascended to heaven, and for those who will believe in Him, He will give them the new birth and will give them the Spirit to live in them. One day, Christ will return, judge all men's deeds, and dwell forever with all those who believed.*

Intermediate (Ages 6–12)

66 **1. Who made you?**
◇ God.

66 **2. What else did God make?**
◇ God made all things.

66 **3. Why did God make all things?**
◇ For His own glory.

66 **4. Why do things work as they do?**
◇ God has so decreed it.

66 **5. How do we learn about God?**
◇ God reveals Himself.

66 **6. Where does God reveal Himself?**
◇ In His word, nature, dreams, and visions.

66 **7. What does God reveal in nature?**
◇ His character, law, and wrath.

66 **8. What more is revealed in His word?**
◇ God's mercy toward His people.

66 **9. Where is God's word found?**
◇ The Bible is God's word.

66 **10. How many Gods are there?**
◇ God is one: God the Father, God the Son, God the Holy Spirit.

11. Where is God?

◇ *He is everywhere.*

12. How long has God existed?

◇ *He has always been.*

13. Who is God?

◇ *God is the first and best of all beings.*

14. What is God like?

◇ *God is a spirit, is eternal, and is a personal being. He is perfect in holiness and is all-powerful and all-knowing.*

15. How does God relate to creation?

◇ *God is the creator, redeemer, preserver, and ruler of the universe.*

16. Who wrote the Bible?

◇ *Obedient men who were led by God the Holy Spirit.*

17. What does it mean to give glory?

◇ *To show honor and enjoy God as the greatest.*

18. Why should you glorify God?

◇ *Because He alone deserves glory.*

19. Can you see God?

◇ *No, I cannot see God, but He always sees me.*

20. Does God know all things?

◇ *Yes, nothing can be hidden from God.*

21. Can God do all things?

◇ *Yes, God is in heaven and does as He pleases.*

22. What does it mean that God is sovereign?

✧ *God has the right, power, and authority to govern all things.*

23. What does it mean that God is holy?

✧ *God is set apart from all other beings. He is perfect and pure.*

24. What does it mean that God is just?

✧ *God always does what is right.*

25. Where do you learn how to love and obey God?

✧ *In the Bible alone through His Spirit.*

26. What did God use to create everything?

✧ *God created everything out of nothing.*

27. How is man unique?

✧ *He bears God's image.*

28. Who was the first man?

✧ *Adam.*

29. Who were our first parents?

✧ *Adam and Eve.*

30. What was Adam like at creation?

✧ *He was good.*

31. Did Adam remain good?

✧ *No, he sinned.*

32. Of what were our first parents made?

✧ *God made the body of Adam out of the ground and formed Eve from the body of Adam.*

Catechism

❝ **33. What did God give Adam and Eve besides bodies?**

◇ *He gave them souls that could never die.*

❝ **34. What is your soul?**

◇ *The part of me that lives forever.*

❝ **35. Who tempted them to sin?**

◇ *The devil deceived Eve. Adam willingly ate the fruit Eve gave him instead of obeying God.*

❝ **36. What came into the world through sin?**

◇ *Death.*

❝ **37. Did Adam act for himself alone?**

◇ *No, he represented all mankind.*

❝ **38. What is sin?**

◇ *Any thought or deed that doesn't bring God glory.*

❝ **39. What is the penalty for sin?**

◇ *Death.*

❝ **40. What did Adam's sin bring?**

◇ *Death came to all men.*

❝ **41. How did Adam's sin affect all men?**

◇ *We all sinned in Adam.*

❝ **42. Must all men die for sin?**

◇ *No, God elected some to life.*

❝ **43. How may we be saved from sin and death?**

◇ *Only through faith in Jesus Christ.*

44. Who is Jesus Christ?

✧ *The eternal Son of God.*

45. Did Jesus ever sin?

✧ *No, only He is righteous.*

46. What did Jesus do for His people?

✧ *He conquered sin and death.*

47. How did He conquer sin and death?

✧ *He absorbed God's wrath for sin by dying then rising again.*

48. What else did Christ conquer?

✧ *All his enemies.*

49. Are His enemies powerful?

✧ *They have come to nothing.*

50. What did He give to His people?

✧ *His own righteousness.*

51. What did He take from His people?

✧ *All their sin.*

52. How is Christ's work brought to His people?

✧ *By the Holy Spirit.*

53. What does the Holy Spirit do?

✧ *He gives life through faith.*

54. What is faith?

✧ *Complete trust in what God says because of who He is.*

55. How do we recognize true faith?

✧ *It yields good works.*

Catechism

56. Who are God's children?

✧ *Those who love and trust Jesus.*

57. What are all God's children called when they gather?

✧ *The church.*

58. What are the traits of His church?

✧ *Love for one another.*

59. Who is head of the church?

✧ *Jesus Christ.*

60. Is His church perfect?

✧ *No, it is being perfected.*

61. When will it be perfect?

✧ *After Christ's return.*

62. What happens to the earth when Christ returns?

✧ *God creates a new heaven and earth.*

63. What happens to men when Christ returns?

✧ *Christ judges all men's deeds.*

64. What happens to those Christ deems righteous?

✧ *They dwell with Him forever.*

65. What happens to those Christ condemns?

✧ *They perish forever.*

66. How do we know we are God's children?

✧ *The Spirit of God bears witness with our spirit that we are children of God.*

67. Who can give a sinner a new heart?

✧ *The Holy Spirit alone.*

66 68. What is getting this new heart called?

✧ *Regeneration.*

66 69. Can anyone earn salvation?

✧ *None can earn it.*

66 70. Why can none be saved through works?

✧ *Because all have sinned and are already condemned to death.*

66 71. Did our Lord Jesus Christ ever commit the least sin?

✧ *No, he is perfectly righteous.*

66 72. How could the Son of God suffer?

✧ *Christ, the Son of God, became a man that He might obey and suffer in our nature.*

66 73. What is meant by the atonement?

✧ *Christ's satisfying divine justice in order to cover the sins of God's children.*

66 74. What is justification?

✧ *It is God's forgiving sinners and declaring them righteous in Christ.*

66 75. What is sanctification?

✧ *It is God's making sinners holy in heart and conduct like His Son.*

66 76. For whom did Christ obey and suffer?

✧ *For those whom the Father had given Him.*

66 77. What kind of death did Christ die?

✧ *The painful and shameful death of the cross.*

66 78. Who will be saved?

✧ *Only those who believe in Jesus Christ.*

66 79. What does it mean to repent?

✧ *To turn from our ways to follow God's ways.*

Catechism

80. What does it mean to believe or have faith in Christ?

◇ *To trust in Christ alone for salvation.*

81. Can you repent and believe in Christ by your own power?

◇ *No, I can do nothing good without the help of God the Holy Spirit.*

82. What tribe was Jesus from?

◇ *As prophesied, the Messiah came from the tribe of Judah.*

83. Who were Jesus's mother and father?

◇ *Jesus was born to Mary and adopted as a son by her husband Joseph.*

84. How many offices does Christ have?

◇ *Christ has three offices.*

85. What are they?

◇ *The offices of prophet, priest, and king.*

86. How is Christ a prophet?

◇ *Christ proclaims to us the will of God.*

87. How is Christ a priest?

◇ *Christ died for our sins and pleads with God for us.*

88. How is Christ a king?

◇ *Christ rules over us and defends us.*

89. How many commandments did God give Israel on Mount Sinai?

◇ *613.*

90. What do we call the commandments God wrote on stone?

◇ *The ten commandments.*

91. What do the first four commandments teach?

◇ *Our duty to God.*

❝ 92. What do the last six commandments teach?

◇ *Our duty to our fellow men.*

❝ 93. What is the sum of the ten commandments?

◇ *To love God with all my heart, soul, mind, and strength, and my neighbor as myself.*

❝ 94. What is the first commandment?

◇ *You shall have no other gods before me.*

❝ 95. What does the first commandment teach us?

◇ *To worship God alone.*

❝ 96. What is the second commandment?

◇ *You shall not make for yourself a carved image.*

❝ 97. What does the second commandment teach us?

◇ *To worship God alone and flee idolatry.*

❝ 98. What is the third commandment?

◇ *You shall not take the name of the Lord your God in vain.*

❝ 99. What does the third commandment teach us?

◇ *To reverence God's name, words, and works.*

❝ 100. What is the fourth commandment?

◇ *Remember the Sabbath day to keep it holy.*

❝ 101. What does the fourth commandment teach us?

◇ *To rest and remember how God has delivered us.*

❝ 102. What is the fifth commandment?

◇ *Honor your father and your mother that your days may be long in the land, which the Lord God is giving you.*

Catechism

103. What does the fifth commandment teach us?
◇ *To embrace God's wisdom in choosing my parents and to love His ways.*

104. What is the sixth commandment?
◇ *You shall not murder.*

105. What does the sixth commandment teach us?
◇ *To value life and flee from angry passions.*

106. What is the seventh commandment?
◇ *You shall not commit adultery.*

107. What does the seventh commandment teach us?
◇ *To be pure in heart and hold fast to our spouse.*

108. What is the eighth commandment?
◇ *You shall not steal.*

109. What does the eighth commandment teach us?
◇ *To be honest, industrious, and respect the possessions of others.*

110. What is the ninth commandment?
◇ *You shall not bear false witness against your neighbor.*

111. What does the ninth commandment teach us?
◇ *To tell the truth regardless of the consequences and flee dishonest gain.*

112. What is the tenth commandment?
◇ *You shall not covet.*

113. What does the tenth commandment teach us?
◇ *To be content with what we have.*

114. Can any man keep God's commandments perfectly?

✧ *Except Christ, no man since the fall of Adam ever did or can keep God's commandments perfectly.*

115. Of what use are the ten commandments to us?

✧ *They reveal God's ways and show our need of a Savior.*

116. What is prayer?

✧ *Prayer is talking to God to worship Him; express thankfulness, needs, and desires; and confess our sins.*

117. In whose name should we pray?

✧ *Only in the name of Christ.*

118. What has Christ given us to teach us how to pray?

✧ *The Lord's Prayer.*

119. Repeat the Lord's Prayer.

✧ *Our Father which art in heaven, Hallowed be thy name. Thy kingdom come, Thy will be done in earth, as it is in heaven. Give us this day our daily bread. And forgive us our debts, as we forgive our debtors. And lead us not into temptation, but deliver us from evil: For thine is the kingdom, and the power, and the glory, for ever. Amen (Matt. 6:9–13 KJU).*

120. How many sacraments are there?

✧ *Two.*

121. What are they?

✧ *Baptism and the Lord's Supper.*

122. Who appointed these sacraments?

✧ *The Lord Jesus Christ.*

Catechism

❝ **123. What sign is used in baptism?**
✧ *The immersion (covering) of the body in water.*

❝ **124. What does baptism signify?**
✧ *That we who are cleansed from sin are dead to the world and now alive in Christ.*

❝ **125. In whose name are we baptized?**
✧ *In the name of the Father, and of the Son, and of the Holy Ghost.*

❝ **126. Who are to be baptized?**
✧ *Those whose faith is in Christ alone for salvation.*

❝ **127. What is the Lord's Supper?**
✧ *The eating of bread and drinking of wine in remembrance of the sufferings and death of Christ.*

❝ **128. What does the bread represent?**
✧ *The body of Christ, broken for our sins.*

❝ **129. What does the wine represent?**
✧ *The blood of Christ, shed for our salvation.*

❝ **130. Who should partake of the Lord's Supper?**
✧ *Only those who love and trust Jesus.*

❝ **131. What is spiritual adoption?**
✧ *Adoption is an act of God's free grace where we become God's children and have rights to all privileges as sons and daughters of God..*

❝ **132. What benefits do God's children receive?**
✧ *Assurance of God's love, peace of conscience, joy in the Holy Spirit, increasing grace, and perseverance to the end.*

133. What is marriage's highest purpose?

◇ *To display the gospel to the world.*

134. How should a husband relate to his wife?

◇ *Like Christ relates to His church.*

135. How does Christ relate to His church?

◇ *He gave Himself up for her to make her holy.*

136. How does a husband love his wife like Christ loves His church?

◇ *Only by the power of the Holy Spirit.*

137. How should a wife relate to her husband?

◇ *She submits as unto the Lord.*

138. How does a wife submit to her husband?

◇ *Only by the power of the Holy Spirit.*

139. Did Christ remain in the tomb after His crucifixion?

◇ *No, He rose from the tomb on the third day after His death.*

140. Where is Christ now?

◇ *In heaven, interceding for the saints.*

141. Will Christ come again?

◇ *Yes, at the last day, Christ will come to judge the world.*

142. What is hell?

◇ *A place of dreadful and endless torment created for demons.*

143. What will become of the righteous?

◇ *They will live forever in the presence of God.*

144. What will become of the wicked on the Day of Judgment?

◇ *They shall be cast into hell.*

Catechism

❝ 145. **What is heaven?**
   ◇ *A glorious place where the righteous shall be forever with God and God with them.*

❝ 146. **What do angels do?**
   ◇ *God created all the angels to do His will and to praise His name.*

❝ 147. **What is God's providence toward the angels?**
   ◇ *God by His providence permitted some of the angels, willfully and irrecoverably, to fall into sin and damnation.*

❝ 148. **What are those angels called that God permitted to fall?**
   ◇ *Demons.*

❝ 149. **Who was the angel that God permitted to lead other angels to damnation?**
   ◇ *Lucifer.*

❝ 150. **What did God change Lucifer's name to?**
   ◇ *Satan.*

❝ 151. **What do demons do today?**
   ◇ *Demons attempt to advance the kingdom of Satan and destroy God's elect.*

❝ 152. **What do angels do today?**
   ◇ *Strive to bring God glory by doing all He commands and minister to God's elect.*

❝ 153. **What has God decreed for Satan and his demons?**
   ◇ *They shall be cast into hell for eternity.*

❝ 154. **What is the last enemy to be cast into hell?**
   ◇ *Death.*

155. What shall happen to the earth?

✧ *God will destroy it and make all things new.*

156. What promise does God fulfill to His elect into eternity?

✧ *God will be their God, and they shall be His people.*

157. What is the good news?

✧ *In mercy, God made a way to save sinners through Jesus's life, death, and resurrection.*

(Long Version)

✧ *There is one God who made everything seen and unseen. He made man in His image. He made him good, but man sinned. God would be just if He punished man forever for his sin, but in His infinite mercy, God made a way to save man. He sent Jesus, the eternal Son of God, fully God and fully man, to live a life we should have lived. Jesus suffered and died a death we deserved, but by the power of the Spirit, He was raised from the dead. He ascended to heaven, and for those who will believe in Him, He will give them the new birth and give them the Spirit to live in them. One day, Christ will return, judge all men's deeds, and dwell forever with all those who believed.*

Catechism

Jewish Bible Timeline (Ages 2+)

Catechism

❝ 1. What person did God choose to make a blessing to all nations?
♢ *Abraham*

❝ 2. Was Abraham righteous when God called him?
♢ *No, he worshipped idols.*

❝ 3. When was Abraham declared righteous?
♢ *When the Bible said he believed God.*

❝ 4. What kind of covenant did God make with Abraham?
♢ *An unconditional covenant.*

❝ 5. What is an unconditional covenant?
♢ *A covenant rooted in the faithfulness of God alone.*

❝ 6. What did God promise Abraham in His unconditional covenant?
♢ *God promised Abraham land, that he would have descendants, and that all the families of the earth would be blessed through him.*

❝ 7. What was the name of Abraham's son conceived through the flesh?
♢ *Ishmael, who was conceived by a slave woman.*

❝ 8. What is the name of Abraham's son conceived through the promise of God?
♢ *Isaac, who was conceived by Abraham's wife, Sarah, according to the promise of God.*

❝ 9. What became of Ishmael?
♢ *God said he would become a great nation, but his hand would be against everyone and everyone's hand against him.*

❝ 10. Who was Isaac's firstborn son?

✧ *Esau was the Isaac's firstborn.*

❝ 11. Did Esau get the firstborn blessing?

✧ *No, the younger son Jacob received the blessing through trickery.*

❝ 12. Did Jacob need to resort to trickery to get the firstborn blessing?

✧ *No, God had already promised that the older son would serve the younger.*

❝ 13. What did God change Jacob's name to?

✧ *Israel.*

❝ 14. What does the name Israel mean?

✧ *One who wrestles with God.*

❝ 15. How many sons did Jacob have?

✧ *He had 12 sons.*

❝ 16. Which of Jacob's sons was sold into slavery by his brothers?

✧ *Joseph.*

❝ 17. Why did Joseph's brothers sell him into slavery?

✧ *Jacob loved Joseph more, and it made his brothers jealous.*

❝ 18. Where did Joseph end up after being sold by his brothers?

✧ *Joseph was enslaved in Egypt.*

❝ 19. What did Joseph's brothers do to deceive their father Jacob?

✧ *They dipped Joseph's coat in blood and told Jacob an animal killed him.*

❝ 20. What became of Joseph in Egypt?

✧ *God was with him, and he gained favor with the Pharaoh of Egypt.*

❝ 21. How did Joseph provide food to his family during a famine?

✧ *Pharaoh made Joseph second in charge of all of Egypt, including selling food.*

Catechism

22. Did Joseph's brothers recognize him when they came to buy food?

✧ *No, but Joseph recognized them and treated them roughly before showing mercy.*

23. What became of Jacob's family when they found Joseph in Egypt?

✧ *Jacob and his family moved to Egypt.*

24. What became of God's people in Egypt?

✧ *They multiplied greatly, and Pharaoh enslaved them out of fear.*

25. Who are the 12 tribes of Israel that received a portion of the promised land?

✧ *Rueben, Simeon, Judah, Dan, Naphtali, Gad, Asher, Issachar, Zebulun, Benjamin, Ephraim, and Manasseh.*

26. Which of Jacob's sons received a double blessing?

✧ *Joseph did because his two sons, Manasseh and Ephraim, both received a portion of land in Canaan.*

27. Which of Jacob's sons did not receive a portion of the promised land?

✧ *The tribe of Levi.*

28. What did the tribe of Levi receive instead of land?

✧ *God is Levi's inheritance.*

29. Did Jacob's firstborn son receive the blessing?

✧ *No, Joseph's son Ephraim received the physical blessing, and Judah received the promise that his descendant would rule.*

30. How many years were God's people enslaved in Egypt?

✧ *430 years.*

31. Who did God raise up to deliver the Jewish people?

✧ *Moses, from the tribe of Levi.*

32. Where did Moses grow up?

✧ *Moses was adopted by Pharaoh's daughter and grew up in Egypt.*

33. How many plagues did God send to Egypt before the Jewish people were set free?

✧ *10.*

34. What was the final plague?

✧ *The death of the firstborn.*

35. Why did the Jewish children not die?

✧ *They obeyed God, sacrificed a lamb, and placed the blood over their doors.*

36. Did the Jewish people leave Egypt in poverty?

✧ *No, God had the Egyptians give them great wealth.*

37. What did the Jewish people do with that wealth?

✧ *They joyfully gave it to build God's temple.*

38. What did God give to Moses on Mt. Sinai?

✧ *The Torah (Law).*

39. Did Israel agree to keep the Torah?

✧ *Yes.*

40. What did God promise to do if Israel did not keep their promise?

✧ *To curse them and remove them from the land He promised Abraham.*

41. Did Israel keep the promise to obey the Torah (Law)?

✧ *No, so they were sent into exile as God promised.*

42. Did God only promise exile if they disobeyed him?

✧ *No, he also promised to bring the nation of Israel back to their land.*

Catechism

❝ 43. Did God choose Israel because they were the best nation?
◇ *No, God chose them because it gave Him pleasure.*

❝ 44. How many feasts did God give Israel?
◇ *Seven feasts or appointed times.*

❝ 45. Are Gentiles required to keep the feasts?
◇ *No, they were only for the tribes of Israel.*

❝ 46. What are the spring feasts?
◇ *Passover, Feast of Unleavened Bread, Firstfruits, and Feast of Weeks (also called Pentecost).*

❝ 47. What are the fall feasts?
◇ *Feast of Trumpets, Day of Atonement, and Feast of Tabernacles (also called Booths).*

❝ 48. What do we learn from the Passover feast?
◇ *Death passed over the firstborn of Jewish families, so God can deliver from death. And the Passover lamb pointed to Jesus.*

❝ 49. What can we learn from the Feast of Unleavened Bread?
◇ *Sin is the problem, and it needs to be removed. Jesus is the bread of life without sin. In Christ, believers are cleansed from sin.*

❝ 50. What can we learn from the Feast of Firstfruits?
◇ *God is the one who gives the harvest, and Jesus is the firstfruit of those who will rise from the dead.*

❝ 51. What can we learn from the Feast of Weeks (Pentecost)?
◇ *Fifty days after the Feast of Firstfruits, God gave the Torah, and 50 days after Jesus rose from the dead, God gave the Holy Spirit.*

❝ 52. What is special about the fall feasts?
◇ *Each teaches a past lesson and a future lesson.*

❝ 53. What can we learn from the Feast of Trumpets?

✧ Israel celebrates the New Year, the birth of creation. One day, the trumpet will sound, and Jesus will come for his church.

❝ 54. What can we learn from the Day of Atonement?

✧ It was the one day a year when the high priest entered the Holy of Holies to make atonement for Israel, and it is the future day when Christ will physically return to earth.

❝ 55. What can we learn from the Feast of Tabernacles (Booths)?

✧ God provided in the wilderness when Israel left Egypt. One day, believers will dwell with God.

❝ 56. What is Jubilee?

✧ Every 50 years, liberty was proclaimed throughout all the land. All the property held by unpaid debts was returned, and all captives were released.

❝ 57. What did Moses do when Israel reached the border of the promised land?

✧ He sent 12 spies to spy out the land God was giving them.

❝ 58. What report did the 12 spies give who were sent out by Moses to inspect the promised land?

✧ Ten spies reported in fear, and two reported with faith in God.

❝ 59. What are the names of the two spies who reported in faith?

✧ Joshua, son of Nun, and Caleb from the tribe of Judah.

❝ 60. What did God do when the people listened to the 10 fearful spies?

✧ God made Israel wander in the wilderness for 40 years.

❝ 61. Did Moses lead Israel into the promised land?

✧ No, he disobeyed God and did not get to enter the promised land.

Catechism

66 62. Who led Israel into the promised land?

♦ *Joshua, son of Nun, led Israel into the promised land.*

66 63. Did Israel drive out all the people dwelling in the promised land?

♦ *No, after Joshua died, the next generation did not follow God and lost their battles.*

66 64. What person did God send to help guide Israel after Joshua died?

♦ *God sent judges who temporarily guided and delivered Israel from its enemies.*

66 65. Name some judges from the Bible.

♦ *Gideon, Deborah, Samson, and Samuel were all judges.*

66 66. Who was Samuel?

♦ *Samuel was the last judge and the prophet who anointed Israel's first king.*

66 67. How did Israel reject God as their ruler?

♦ *Israel asked for a king like the other nations.*

66 68. Who was Israel's first king?

♦ *God gave Saul from the tribe of Benjamin as Israel's first king.*

66 69. Who was Israel's second king?

♦ *David from the tribe of Judah.*

66 70. What did God promise King David?

♦ *God promised David that someone from his family line would be the Messiah, and His kingdom would endure forever.*

66 71. Which of David's sons was his successor as king?

♦ *Solomon, son of Bathsheba whose husband, Uriah, David had killed.*

66 72. Who built the temple in Jerusalem?

♦ *God let Solomon build it since David was a man of blood.*

73. Did Solomon remain faithful?

✧ *No, Solomon did not heed God's instruction and was led into idolatry by foreign women.*

74. What consequence came as a result of Solomon's idolatry?

✧ *The kingdom was divided into two: the Northern Kingdom and the Southern Kingdom.*

75. How many tribes were in the Northern Kingdom?

✧ *10 tribes.*

76. What two tribes stayed faithful to David's line of rule?

✧ *The tribe of Benjamin and Judah.*

77. What was the capital city of the Northern Kingdom?

✧ *Samaria.*

78. What was the capital city of the Southern Kingdom?

✧ *Jerusalem was, is, and will always be the Holy City.*

79. Why were both kingdoms conquered?

✧ *Because of their continued idolatry, God scattered them as He promised He would.*

80. What year was the Northern Kingdom conquered by the Assyrians?

✧ *722 B.C.*

81. What year was the Southern Kingdom conquered by the Babylonians?

✧ *It was conquered in 607, and the temple was destroyed in 586 B.C.*

82. What other names does the Bible call the Northern Kingdom?

✧ *Ephraim and the House of Israel.*

83. What other name does the Bible call the Southern Kingdom?

✧ *Judah.*

Catechism

84. How many kings ruled the Northern Kingdom?

✧ *God anointed 19 kings, but they were all evil, and none of them were from David's line.*

85. How many kings ruled the Southern Kingdom?

✧ *God anointed 20 kings; six were good, and all were from David's line.*

86. Did the tribes of Israel ever return to the land God promised them?

✧ *As God prophesied, Cyrus, king of Persia, let the Southern Kingdom exiles return to Israel. Many of the tribes of the Northern Kingdom returned, but not in the same prophetic manner.*

87. Who was Elijah?

✧ *A prophet during wicked King Ahab's reign who performed many miracles and destroyed the prophets of Baal.*

88. What did Ezekiel the prophet prophesy about?

✧ *Ezekiel warned of Israel's destruction but promised a new spirit would be given and that God would reunify Israel.*

89. What did Isaiah prophesy?

✧ *Isaiah warned of Judah's destruction but gave many prophesies about the coming Messiah.*

90. Who is Ezra?

✧ *A priestly descendant of Aaron who returned after the Babylonian exile and reintroduced the Torah (law) to Israel.*

91. Who led the first return of the Jews from exile?

✧ *Zerubbabel led the first group of Jews back to Jerusalem after 70 years of exile and rebuilt the temple.*

92. Who led the second return of the Jews from exile?

◇ *Ezra the scribe led the second group of Jews back to Jerusalem and restored temple worship.*

93. Who led the third return of the Jews from exile?

◇ *Nehemiah led the third group of Jewish people back and rebuilt the temple wall.*

94. Led by Nehemiah, how long did it take to rebuild the wall in Jerusalem?

◇ *It only took 52 days.*

95. Why was the second temple not as good as the first?

◇ *It was without the ark of the covenant, so God's presence was not there like before.*

96. Who is Esther?

◇ *A young Jewish girl who become queen of Persia during the exile.*

97. What did Esther do?

◇ *Queen Esther listened to wise counsel, risked her life, and stopped a plan to exterminate all Jews.*

98. Who was Malachi?

◇ *Malachi was the final prophet God sent to Israel before sending John the Baptist 400 years later.*

99. Who was John the Baptist?

◇ *John the Baptist was the last Old Testament prophet and the forerunner of the Messiah.*

100. What did John the Baptist say when Jesus approached him?

◇ *"Behold, the Lamb of God, who takes away the sin of the world!" (John 1:29).*

Family Discipleship Tools

Scripture Blessings

These blessings are simply scriptures that have been somewhat personalized so a father, mother, grandparents, or even older siblings can pray them over the children.

Genesis 48:15–16*

May the God before whom Abraham and Isaac walked,
   the God who has been my shepherd to this day,
   and who has delivered me from all harm
   bless you and make His name live on in you
   and in your children after you. Amen!

1 Kings 8:57–60*

May the Lord our God be with you as He has been with me.
May He never leave or forsake you.
May He incline your heart toward Him
   and cause you to walk in all His ways.
Day and night may your prayers be near Him.
May the Lord maintain your cause
   and the cause of all His people
So that you and all the peoples of the earth may know
   that the Lord is God, and there is none other! Amen!

Numbers 6:24–26*

The Lord will bless you and keep you.
The Lord will make His face shine on you
   and be gracious unto you.
The Lord will lift up His countenance upon you
   and give you peace. Amen!

Psalm 1*

May the Lord bless you!
May the Lord give you
   the courage not to walk in the counsel of the wicked;
   the faith not to stand in the path of sinners;
   and the resolve not to sit in the seat of mockers.
May you always delight in the law of the Lord
   and meditate on it day and night.
May you be like a tree planted by streams of water,
   which yields its fruit in season
   and whose leaf does not wither.
May the Lord prosper all that you do for His glory,
And may the Lord watch over your way
   all the days of your life
   so that you can stand in the day of judgment
   and join the assembly of the righteous forever. Amen!

Deuteronomy 28:3–6*

Blessed shall you be when you obey the Lord your God.
Blessed shall you be in the city.
Blessed shall you be in the country.

Tools

Blessed shall be your offspring.
Blessed shall be the work of your hands.
Blessed shall you be when you come in.
Blessed shall you be when you go out.
Blessed be the name of the Lord in your life, forever and ever. Amen!

Psalm 4*

May the Lord answer when you pray
   and relieve you in distress.
May He lift up the light of His countenance upon you
   and put gladness in your heart exceeding all earthly joy.
May the Lord establish you as a godly man/woman
   who trusts in Him.
May the Lord make you dwell in safety.
And when you lie down, may you sleep in peace. Amen!

Psalm 13:5–6*

May the Lord deal bountifully with you
   all the days of your life,
And may you always trust in the lovingkindness of the Lord.
In the days of sorrow and darkness,
   may you rejoice in the Lord's salvation
And sing to Him forever and ever. Amen!

Philippians 1:9–11

I bless you, that your love may abound more and more
   in real knowledge and all discernment,

so that you may approve the things that are excellent,
  in order to be sincere and blameless until the day of Christ;
May you be filled with the fruit of righteousness
  which comes through Jesus Christ, to the glory and praise of God.
Amen!

1 Thessalonians 3:10–13*

May God complete what is lacking in your faith
  so you will know God the Father, His Son Jesus
  so the Spirit of God will direct your way.
May the Lord cause you to increase and abound in love for all people,
  so that He may establish your heart without blame in holiness
  before God at the coming of the Lord Jesus. Amen!

Psalm 16*

May the Lord be your counselor all the days of your life.
Even in the night, may the Lord instruct your heart.
May you always set the Lord before you.
May the Lord always be at your right hand
  so that you will never be shaken.
May your heart be glad, your tongue rejoice,
  and your body rest secure.
May the Lord make known to you the path of life,
  fill you with joy in His presence,
  and give you pleasures at His right hand forever and ever. Amen!

Tools

Psalm 23*

May the LORD be your shepherd.
May He bless you with all that you need.
May He make you lie down in green pastures,
    lead you beside quiet waters, and restore your soul.
May He guide you in paths of righteousness
    for His name's sake.
May His rod and staff comfort you so that you fear no evil
    even when you walk
      through the valley of the shadow of death.
May the Lord prepare a table before you
    in the presence of your enemies.
May He anoint your head with oil.
May your cup of joy overflow continuously.
May the Lord's goodness and mercy follow you
    all the days of your life.
And may you dwell in the house of the Lord forever. Amen!

Psalm 103:1–5*

May you bless the Lord all the days of your life.
With all that is within you, may you bless His holy name.
May you never forget the benefits of Him who
    forgives your sins, heals your diseases, and
    redeems your life from destruction.
May the Lord satisfy your years with good things
    and crown your life with lovingkindness
    and tender mercies forever. Amen!

Tools

Psalm 112*

May you be a blessed man/woman who fears the Lord;
May you find great delight in the Lord's commands.
May your children be mighty in the land. Even to the next
    generation, may you and your children be blessed.
May you find your wealth and your riches in God.
May you endure in righteousness forever.
Even in darkness may the light dawn for you.
May you be a gracious, compassionate
    and righteous man/woman.
May you never be shaken. And may your name, [Insert Name],
    be remembered by the Lord forever. Amen!

Psalm 121:5–8*

May the Lord watch over you.
May He be a shade at your right hand
    so that the sun will not harm you by day
    or the moon by night.
May the Lord keep you from all harm.
May He watch over your life.
May He watch over your coming and your going
    both now and forever. Amen!

2 Thessalonians 1:11–12*

To this end I bless you in the name of the Lord:
That the Lord may make you worthy of His calling
    fulfilling every good resolve and work of faith

by His power.
And may the name of the Lord Jesus be glorified in you
    and you in Him, according to the grace
    of our God and our Lord Jesus Christ,
    to whom be glory forever and ever. Amen!

2 Thessalonians 2:16–17, 3:16*

May the Lord Jesus Christ Himself and God our Father,
    who loves you and by His grace
    gives you eternal encouragement and hope, comfort
    and strengthen your heart in every good deed and word.
May the Lord of peace give you peace continually
    and in every good circumstance.
And may the grace of the Lord Jesus Christ be with you
    now and forever. Amen!

Hebrews 12:1*

May the Lord bless you like the mighty men and women of faith
    who have gone before you.
May He give you:
    grace to lay aside every encumbrance
    and the sin which so easily entangles us;
    endurance to run the race set before you;
    and eyes fixed on Jesus,
    who is the author and perfecter of faith! Amen!

Hebrews 13:20–21*

May the God of peace
   who brought up from the dead Jesus Christ our Lord
   through the blood of the eternal covenant
   equip you with every good thing to do His will,
   and work in you that which is pleasing in His sight
   through the power of Jesus Christ
   to whom be the glory forever and ever. Amen!

Psalm 125:1–2*

May the Lord increase your confidence in Him.
May you be like Mount Zion which cannot be shaken
   but endures forever.
As the mountains surround Jerusalem,
   may the Lord surround you
   both now and forever. Amen!

Psalm 15*

May you be blessed with the abiding presence of the Lord.
May your walk be blameless and your work be righteous.
May the Lord keep your tongue from sin
   and your relationships pure.
May you be honorable, loving, and generous with your money.
May the Lord keep you in His way
   so that you will not be shaken
   but endure in righteousness forever. Amen!

Romans 15:13*

May the God of hope fill you with all joy and peace
   as you trust in Him,
   so that you may abound in hope,
   through the power of the Holy Spirit. Amen!

2 Corinthians 13:14*

May the grace of the Lord Jesus Christ and the love of God
   and the fellowship of the Holy Spirit abide with you
   now and forever. Amen!

Ephesians 3:14–19*

And now, may our great and eternal Father bless you.
May He strengthen your inner being
   with power from the Holy Spirit.
May Christ dwell in your heart through faith.
May you be rooted and grounded in love
   so you will comprehend with all the saints
   the breadth and length and height and depth
   of the love of Christ, which surpasses knowledge.
May you be filled up to all the fullness of God
   according to the riches of His glory.
And may you exalt His glorious name forever and ever.
Amen!

Tools

Ephesians 3:20–21*

May God do for you exceeding abundantly
   beyond all that you ask or think,
   according to the power that works within you,
To Him be the glory
   in your life in Christ Jesus,
   and to all your lineage forever and ever. Amen!

Ephesians 6:10–17*

May you be a man/woman who is strong in the Lord
   and in His mighty power.
May you be blessed with the full armor of God
   so that you can resist the devil's schemes.
May you stand firm with the belt of truth
   buckled around your waist, and the breastplate
   of righteousness in place, and your feet
   fitted with the preparation of the gospel of peace.
May you take up the shield of faith, the helmet of salvation,
   and the sword of the Spirit, which is the word of God,
   so that when the day of evil comes,
   you will be able to stand your ground. Amen!

Ephesians 1:17–19

May the God of our Lord Jesus Christ, the Father of glory,
   give you the Spirit of wisdom and of revelation
   in the knowledge of Him.
And may the eyes of your heart be enlightened

Tools

so you will know what is the hope to which he has called you,
the riches of his glorious inheritance in the saints,
and the immeasurable greatness of his power. Amen!

1 Thessalonians 5:23–24*

May the God of peace sanctify you through and through.
May your whole spirit, soul, and body be preserved
without blame at the coming of our Lord Jesus Christ.
And may you always trust the One who calls you
and who has faithfully accomplished your redemption. Amen!

Psalms 51:1–2

May God have mercy on you according to his steadfast love,
according to his abundant mercy.
And may he blot out your transgressions.
May our mighty God wash you thoroughly from
your iniquity and cleanse you from all sin. Amen!

Psalm 51: 9–12

May God hide his face from your sin
and blot out all of your iniquities.
May God create in you a clean heart,
and renew your spirit from within.
May you never be cast away from God's presence.
May God give you the fullness of His Spirit,
restore the joy of your salvation
and uphold you with a willing spirit. Amen!

Tools

Deuteronomy 13:3–4

When the LORD God tests you to know
   whether you will follow Him with all your heart and soul,
May you walk after God, fear Him, keep His commandments,
   obey His voice.
May you serve Him and hold fast to Him all the days of your life. Amen!

Deuteronomy 31:6

May you be strong and courageous.
May you never fear or be in dread of any man
   because He goes with you
And may God never leave you or forsake you. Amen!

1 Timothy 4:12–13

May no one despise you because of your youth, but instead
   may you set the believers an example in speech,
   in conduct, in love, in faith, in purity.
May your life be marked with a devotion to the reading of scripture,
   exhorting and teaching others. Amen!

Ecclesiastes 3:1–8

I bless you with knowing that your Father's appointed time
   for everything in your life is beautiful.
I bless you with trusting His sovereign plan, even when you can't see it.
I bless you with joy in births, peace surrounding death,
   comfort during times of weeping, friends to laugh with,

Tools

wisdom to know when to gather, wisdom to know when to scatter,
    boldness to speak, strength to be silent, resolve to fight when needed,
    and may your heart rest during times of peace. Amen!

Psalms 91: 9–16

I bless you with the Lord as your dwelling place
    and in whom you find refuge.
May no evil befall you, may no sickness come near you.
May God's angels guard all your ways.
May you trample on all enemies that seem as strong as a lion
    or dangerous as a snake because God holds fast to you in love
    and will always deliver you.
I bless you with God's protection because He knows your name,
    answers when you call, gives you long life, satisfies you,
    and reveals to you His salvation. Amen!

John 17:14–17

Father, I have given these children your word,
    and if the world hates them because they are not of the world,
I do not ask that you take them out of the world,
    but that you keep them from the evil one.
Sanctify them in the truth; your word is truth. Amen!

1 Timothy 6:11–14

I bless you to pursue righteousness, godliness,
    faith, love, steadfastness, and gentleness.
I bless you to fight the good fight of the faith;

to take hold of the eternal life that calls out to you
and that you would make the good confession
in the presence of many witnesses.
I bless you in the presence of God, who gives life to all things,
and of Christ Jesus, to keep the commandments unstained
and free from reproach until the appearing of our Lord Jesus Christ. Amen!

Proverbs 3:5–8

May you be blessed to trust in the Lord with all your heart,
and not lean on your own understanding.
May you acknowledge him in all your ways.
May the Lord make your paths straight.
I bless you to not be wise in your own eyes
but instead to fear the Lord and turn away from evil,
bringing healing to your flesh and refreshment to your bones. Amen!

Proverbs 3:9–12

May you honor the LORD with your wealth
and with the firstfruits of what you produce.
May the Lord then fill your barns with plenty
so that your vats will be bursting with wine.
My son/daughter, may you never despise the Lord's discipline
or be weary of His reproof, but see the Lord's reproof
as assurance of His love and delight in you. Amen!

Tools

Philippians 4:8–9

I bless you to think on these things; whatever is true,
  whatever is honorable, whatever is just, whatever is pure,
  whatever is lovely, whatever is commendable,
  if there is any excellence, if there is anything worthy of praise.
And may you practice these things as I try to live them before you
  so that the God of peace will be with you. Amen!

Ephesians 4:29–32

I bless your tongue that no corrupting talk will come out of your mouth,
  but only such as is good for building up, as fits the occasion,
  that it may give grace to those who hear.
And may you never grieve the Holy Spirit of God,
  by whom you were sealed for the day of redemption.
I bless you with a heart that puts away all bitterness and wrath
  and anger and clamor, slander, along with all malice,
That you would be kind to all, tenderhearted, forgiving others,
  as God in Christ forgives you. Amen!

Colossians 1:9–11

I bless you that you will be filled with the knowledge of God's will
  in all spiritual wisdom and understanding,
  so you will walk in a manner worthy of the Lord.
May you please God by bearing fruit in every good work
  and increase in the knowledge of God.
May God strengthen you with all power,
  according to his glorious might, for all endurance
  and patience with joy.

Tools

Colossians 1:12–13

I give thanks to the Father, who has qualified you
  to share in the inheritance of the saints in light.
I thank God that He will deliver you from
  the domain of darkness and transfer you to
  the kingdom of his beloved Son,
  in whom you may receive redemption,
  the forgiveness of sins. Amen!

1 Thessalonians 3:11–13

May our God and Father himself
  and our Lord Jesus direct your way.
And may the Lord make you increase
  and abound in love for all,
  so that he may establish your heart
  blameless in holiness. Amen!

Exodus 33:13

I bless you with favor in God's sight
  so he will show you His ways,
That you may know Him. Amen!

Psalm 91:14–16

I bless you with the ability to hold fast to God in love
  so He will deliver you.
May God protect you, because He knows your name.

Tools

When you call to Him, He will answer
  and when you are in trouble, He will be with you and rescue you.
May God bless you with long life,
  satisfy you, and show you His salvation. Amen!

Jonah 2:2

I bless you so that when you call out in your distress,
God will answer you.
And when you cry out to him,
He will hear your voice. Amen!

Joshua 1:5–6

I bless you that no man shall be able to stand before you
  all the days of your life.
May God be with you as He was with Moses,
  and may he never leave you or forsake you.
I bless you to be strong and courageous,
  to inherit all God has for you. Amen!

Joshua 1:7–8

May you be strong and very courageous, being careful
  to do according to all God asks of you
  and not to turn from it to the right hand or to the left,
  that you may have good success wherever you go.
May His word never depart from your mouth,
  but you shall meditate on it day and night,
  so that you will be careful to do all that is written.

Tools

For then He will make your way prosperous,
and then you will have good success. Amen!

Genesis 48:20 (for boys)

May God make you like Ephraim and Manasseh. Amen!

Proverbs 31:25–26, 29 (for girls)

May strength and dignity be your clothing as you laugh
at the days to come.
May you open your mouth with wisdom as the teaching of
kindness is on your tongue.
As girls all around you do well, I bless you to surpass them all.
Amen!

* These blessings are copied or adapted from *A Father's Guide to Blessing His Children* by David Michael.

Tools

Family Dictionary

....

Adoption – when God chooses to bring those who love and trust Jesus into His family and gives them His Spirit

Altar – a platform used to offer a sacrifice

Angel – a spirit created to serve God's purposes

Authority – the right to be in charge

Baptize – to immerse (cover) in water (a way of identifying with Jesus's death, burial, and resurrection)

Compassion – to see, care, and act when others are in need

Confess – to tell the truth about your sin without being asked

Confidence – sure and firm hope; believing and relying on God

Delight – when hearts are happy because God is in the highest place

Demon – an angel who chose to follow Satan instead of serving God

Devil – another name for Satan

Disciple – a person who does the things his teacher teaches no matter the cost

Discipline – God lovingly training His children to be more like Jesus

Eternity – without beginning or end

Exile – to be sent away from a certain place

Faith – Complete trust in what God says because of who He is

Fast – to not eat food or to eat only certain foods for a limited time

Generous – to joyfully and abundantly give to others

Glorify – to show, honor, and enjoy God as the greatest

God's children – those who love and trust Jesus

Grace – when God gives and does good to His children instead of giving what they deserve

Gratitude – being thankful to God no matter what He gives

Heart – where belief lives

Heaven – the place where God lives

Hebrew – a name for someone from the nation of Israel

Hell – a place of eternal fire and separation from God, created for demons

Holy – to be set apart (God is holy, or perfect and separate from sin)

Humility – happy when in the lowest place of importance

Jewish – referring to someone from the nation of Israel

Joy – delight that comes from knowing God no matter what situation one is in

Justice – fairness in giving a reward, discipline, or punishment

Obedience – doing what you're told right away with a great attitude

Patience – waiting without complaining, even when things get hard

Praise – to tell God how good He is

Prayer – conversation with God. We pray to the Father because of Jesus with the help of the Spirit

Pride – showing honor to yourself and enjoying yourself as the greatest

Reconcile – to make peace and remove separation between God and people

Redemption – to be bought back from slavery

Repentance – turning away from your own ways and following God's ways

Righteous – having a clean heart in all you do

Righteousness – to be free from guilt or sin

Sacrifice – a flawless animal, killed upon an altar in order to worship God

Satan – the lead angel who rebelled against God, who now deceives and accuses God's children

Sin – anything that comes from the heart that does not bring glory to God

Sovereign – having the right, power, and authority to be in charge

Soul – the part of a person that lives forever

Temptation – when sin seems good even though it is bad

Thanksgiving – to thank God for what He has done

Trust – to show faith by acting on what you believe

Wisdom – to know what God thinks about something and how to act upon it

Tools

Songs for the Family
(Look any of these up on YouTube. Suggested performer is in parentheses)

"Here Is Love" by William Rees (Bethel Church)

"Amazing Grace" by John Newton (Wintley Phipps)

"The Solid Rock" by Edward Mote (Austin Stone)

"I Stand Amazed" by Charles Gabriel (Chris Tomlin)

"Jesus Paid It All" by Elvina Hall (David Crowder)

"In Christ Alone" by Townend and Getty (Lauren Daigle)

"10,000 Reasons" by Matt Redman and Jonas Myrin

"How Deep the Father's Love for Us" by Stuart Townend (Fernando Ortega)

"Go Tell It on the Mountain" by John W. Work Jr. (MercyMe)

"Doxology" by Thomas Ken (David Crowder Band)

"Joyful, Joyful, We Adore Thee" by Henry Van Dyke (Casting Crowns)

"How Great Thou Art" by Stuart Hine (Carrie Underwood)

Tools

Summary of Old Testament Books

Pentateuch – First five books

- **Genesis** – creation, the fall, the flood, spread of the nations, the beginning of the Hebrew nation, and enslavement of God's people
- **Exodus** – God delivers Israel from bondage; Israel's birth as a nation, God's covenant with Israel, giving of the Torah, and instructions to build the tabernacle
- **Leviticus** – instructions on the sacrificial system and the priesthood, and instructions on moral purity
- **Numbers** – the journey to the promised land; at Mt. Sinai, Israel makes the golden calf; God disciplines the nation with 40 years of wandering in the desert
- **Deuteronomy** – God's commentary on the covenant

Historical Books – 12 books

- **Joshua** – the conquest and the allotting of the promised land of Canaan
- **Judges** – the first 300 years in the promised land and the time of the judges; Israel fails to drive out the people of Canaan, and everyone does what is right in their own eyes
- **Ruth** – the story of the Messianic family of David; Boaz, a kinsman redeemer, redeems a Moabite named Ruth

The next six books trace the time from Samuel to the captivity

- **1 Samuel** – Israel transitions from judges to having a king; the prophet Samuel anoints Saul as king, Saul disobeys, God rejects Saul, and Samuel anoints David

- **2 Samuel** – David's reign as king; David commits adultery and murder; the rise of his son Solomon

- **1 Kings** – Division of the kingdom; Solomon and the nation Israel become powerful and famous; Solomon's idolatry leads to a divided kingdom (10 tribes to the north and two to the south)

- **2 Kings** – History of the divided kingdom; All 19 kings of Israel were bad; in Judah, eight of 20 rulers were good, and the rest were idolatrous; God exiles both kingdoms from the land; Assyrians conquer the North, and Babylon conquers the South.

- **1 Chronicles** – focuses on the genealogies of the Southern Kingdom and recounts much of the books of Samuel and Kings

- **2 Chronicles** – History of the Southern Kingdom of Judah; recounts the life of Solomon, the building of the temple, and of Judah's history

The next three books deal with Israel's restoration.

- **Ezra** – records the Jews' return from the Babylonian exile in two separate groups and the rebuilding of the temple; Zerubbabel led the first group, and Ezra led the second group

- **Nehemiah** – continued story of return of the Jews to Jerusalem; Nehemiah rebuilds the wall of Jerusalem; Ezra reads the Torah (law), and there is a great revival

- **Esther** – while in exile God, delivers His people; Queen Esther, a Hebrew married to a Persian king, listens to wise counsel and risks her life, resulting in the Jews escaping extinction

Tools

Poetical – five books

- **Job** – God in His sovereignty tests a righteous man by allowing him to be directly attacked by Satan; God's mercy is found in Job's deepened relationship with God

- **Psalms** – written mostly by King David, a collection of prayers, songs, and meditations

- **Proverbs** – written mostly by King Solomon, a collection of poems and wise sayings useful in everyday life

- **Ecclesiastes** – summary of King Solomon's search for the meaning of life; he concludes that all is vanity and counsels all to enjoy God's gifts and fear and obey Him

- **Song of Solomon** – poetic song between Solomon and his bride shadowing the love between God and His people

Prophetic – 17 books (major prophets and minor prophets)

Major Prophets – five books

- **Isaiah** – (to Southern Kingdom) proclaims God's coming judgment on the Southern Kingdom by Babylon and gives prophetic insight to the coming Messiah

- **Jeremiah** – (to Southern Kingdom) final plea for Judah's repentance before eventual judgment; prophesies God's plan for a new covenant and the coming king

- **Lamentations** – five poems of painful lament over the desolation of Jerusalem; describes the defeat and fall of Jerusalem

- **Ezekiel** – during Babylonian exile, Ezekiel pronounces judgment on Israel and surrounding nations; Ezekiel provides a vision of the future millennial kingdom and tells of a restoration of a remnant of Israel

- **Daniel** – historic account of how God protected Israel during exile; many visions show God's sovereign power over all the kingdoms of the earth

Minor Prophets – 12 books

- **Hosea** – (Northern Kingdom) Hosea's marriage to an unfaithful wife is a shadow of Israel's unfaithfulness to God and His unfailing love

- **Joel** – (pre-exile Southern Kingdom) a terrifying account of future judgment if Judah does not repent; gives hope of the coming kingdom

- **Amos** – (Northern Kingdom) warned Israel of its coming judgment due to their oppression of the poor and their lack of justice

- **Obadiah** – (Edom) proclaims destruction for Edom, a neighboring Gentile nation, for taking pleasure in God's judgment of Jerusalem

- **Jonah** – (Nineveh) proclaims a coming judgment on Nineveh if they do not repent; Nineveh listens and is spared, to the displeasure of Jonah

- **Micah** – (Northern and Southern Kingdoms) proclaims destruction for Israel and Judah for their idolatry and lack of justice; promises restoration and prophesies that Messiah will be born in Bethlehem

- **Nahum** – (Nineveh) prophesies destruction to Nineveh; Nineveh repented after Jonah's preaching, but their return to wickedness brought the judgment of God

- **Habakkuk** – (Southern Kingdom) questions God for not addressing Judah's wickedness; questions God's use of the Babylonians to judge Judah; with no answer, Habakkuk rests in God's salvation

- **Zephaniah** – (Southern Kingdom) announces the Day of the Lord against Judah and the nations; God will eventually bless the nations, and a remnant of Judah will be restored

- **Haggai** – after returning from exile, Haggai says God is withholding prosperity because they are building their own houses first; the people listen, and God responds with encouragement and blessing

- **Zechariah** – encourages the Jews to complete the temple; contains many messianic prophecies; speaks of Gentiles worshiping God

- **Malachi** – After returning from exile, Malachi delivers a final message of coming judgment to a disobedient people and tells of a forerunner to the Messiah

Scripture Memory Passages

John 1:1–14

[1] In the beginning was the Word, and the Word was with God, and the Word was God. [2] He was in the beginning with God. [3] All things were made through him, and without him was not any thing made that was made. [4] In him was life, and the life was the light of men. [5] The light shines in the darkness, and the darkness has not overcome it.

[6] There was a man sent from God, whose name was John. [7] He came as a witness, to bear witness about the light, that all might believe through him. [8] He was not the light, but came to bear witness about the light.

[9] The true light, which gives light to everyone, was coming into the world. [10] He was in the world, and the world was made through him, yet the world did not know him. [11] He came to his own, and his own people did not receive him. [12] But to all who did receive him, who believed in his name, he gave the right to become children of God, [13] who were born, not of blood nor of the will of the flesh nor of the will of man, but of God.

[14] And the Word became flesh and dwelt among us, and we have seen his glory, glory as of the only Son from the Father, full of grace and truth.

Psalm 23

[1] The LORD is my shepherd; I shall not want.
[2]   He makes me lie down in green pastures.
He leads me beside still waters.
[3]   He restores my soul.
He leads me in paths of righteousness
    for his name's sake.
[4] Even though I walk through the valley of the shadow of death,
    I will fear no evil,
for you are with me;
    your rod and your staff,
    they comfort me.
[5] You prepare a table before me
    in the presence of my enemies;
you anoint my head with oil;
    my cup overflows.
[6] Surely goodness and mercy shall follow me
    all the days of my life,
and I shall dwell in the house of the LORD
    forever.

Psalm 150

[1] Praise the LORD!
Praise God in his sanctuary;
    praise him in his mighty heavens!
[2] Praise him for his mighty deeds;
    praise him according to his excellent greatness!
[3] Praise him with trumpet sound;

Tools

praise him with lute and harp!
4 Praise him with tambourine and dance;
   praise him with strings and pipe!
5 Praise him with sounding cymbals;
   praise him with loud clashing cymbals!
6 Let everything that has breath praise the Lord!
Praise the Lord!

Proverbs 3:1–12

1 My son, do not forget my teaching,
   but let your heart keep my commandments,
2 for length of days and years of life
   and peace they will add to you.
3 Let not steadfast love and faithfulness forsake you;
   bind them around your neck;
   write them on the tablet of your heart.
4 So you will find favor and good success
   in the sight of God and man.
5 Trust in the Lord with all your heart,
   and do not lean on your own understanding.
6 In all your ways acknowledge him,
   and he will make straight your paths.
7 Be not wise in your own eyes;
   fear the Lord, and turn away from evil.
8 It will be healing to your flesh
   and refreshment to your bones.
9 Honor the Lord with your wealth
   and with the firstfruits of all your produce;
10 then your barns will be filled with plenty,

Tools

and your vats will be bursting with wine.
[11] My son, do not despise the LORD's discipline
    or be weary of his reproof,
[12] for the LORD reproves him whom he loves,
    as a father the son in whom he delights.

Psalm 27:1–6

[1] The LORD is my light and my salvation;
    whom shall I fear?
The LORD is the stronghold of my life;
    of whom shall I be afraid?
[2] When evildoers assail me
    to eat up my flesh,
my adversaries and foes,
    it is they who stumble and fall.
[3] Though an army encamp against me,
    my heart shall not fear;
though war arise against me,
    yet I will be confident.
[4] One thing have I asked of the LORD,
    that will I seek after:
that I may dwell in the house of the LORD
    all the days of my life,
to gaze upon the beauty of the LORD
    and to inquire in his temple.
[5] For he will hide me in his shelter
    in the day of trouble;
he will conceal me under the cover of his tent;
    he will lift me high upon a rock.

Tools

[6] And now my head shall be lifted up
    above my enemies all around me,
and I will offer in his tent
    sacrifices with shouts of joy;
I will sing and make melody to the LORD.

Colossians 1:15–20

[15] He is the image of the invisible God, the firstborn of all creation. [16] For by him all things were created, in heaven and on earth, visible and invisible, whether thrones or dominions or rulers or authorities—all things were created through him and for him. [17] And he is before all things, and in him all things hold together. [18] And he is the head of the body, the church. He is the beginning, the firstborn from the dead, that in everything he might be preeminent. [19] For in him all the fullness of God was pleased to dwell, [20] and through him to reconcile to himself all things, whether on earth or in heaven, making peace by the blood of his cross.

Romans 12:9–18

[9] Let love be genuine. Abhor what is evil; hold fast to what is good. [10] Love one another with brotherly affection. Outdo one another in showing honor. [11] Do not be slothful in zeal, be fervent in spirit, serve the Lord. [12] Rejoice in hope, be patient in tribulation, be constant in prayer. [13] Contribute to the needs of the saints and seek to show hospitality.

[14] Bless those who persecute you; bless and do not curse them. [15] Rejoice with those who rejoice, weep with those who weep. [16] Live in harmony with one another. Do not be haughty, but associate with the lowly. Never be

wise in your own sight. [17] Repay no one evil for evil, but give thought to do what is honorable in the sight of all. [18] If possible, so far as it depends on you, live peaceably with all.

Isaiah 53:1–6

[1] Who has believed what he has heard from us?
   And to whom has the arm of the Lord been revealed?
[2] For he grew up before him like a young plant,
   and like a root out of dry ground;
he had no form or majesty that we should look at him,
   and no beauty that we should desire him.
[3] He was despised and rejected by men,
   a man of sorrows and acquainted with grief;
and as one from whom men hide their faces
   he was despised, and we esteemed him not.
[4] Surely he has borne our griefs
   and carried our sorrows;
yet we esteemed him stricken,
   smitten by God, and afflicted.
[5] But he was pierced for our transgressions;
   he was crushed for our iniquities;
upon him was the chastisement that brought us peace,
   and with his wounds we are healed.
[6] All we like sheep have gone astray;
   we have turned—every one—to his own way;
and the Lord has laid on him
   the iniquity of us all.

Tools

Galatians 5:22–23

22 But the fruit of the Spirit is love, joy, peace, patience, kindness, goodness, faithfulness, 23 gentleness, self-control; against such things there is no law.

Romans 8:28–39

28 And we know that for those who love God all things work together for good, for those who are called according to his purpose. 29 For those whom he foreknew he also predestined to be conformed to the image of his Son, in order that he might be the firstborn among many brothers. 30 And those whom he predestined he also called, and those whom he called he also justified, and those whom he justified he also glorified.

31 What then shall we say to these things? If God is for us, who can be against us? 32 He who did not spare his own Son but gave him up for us all, how will he not also with him graciously give us all things? 33 Who shall bring any charge against God's elect? It is God who justifies. 34 Who is to condemn? Christ Jesus is the one who died—more than that, who was raised—who is at the right hand of God, who indeed is interceding for us. 35 Who shall separate us from the love of Christ? Shall tribulation, or distress, or persecution, or famine, or nakedness, or danger, or sword? 36 As it is written,

"For your sake we are being killed all the day long;
we are regarded as sheep to be slaughtered."

37 No, in all these things we are more than conquerors through him who loved us. 38 For I am sure that neither death nor life, nor angels nor rulers, nor things present nor things to come, nor powers, 39 nor height nor depth, nor anything else in all creation, will be able to separate us from the love of God in Christ Jesus our Lord.

Tools

In Conclusion

Final Message to Parents

. . . .

In order to be a foster parent and remain licensed by the state, you must attend various types of training. They range from behavioral management to learning about psychotropic medications. During the course of our time as foster parents, my wife and I attended a nine-week training called Empowered to Connect. Although it was geared toward parents who have children "from hard places," we found it applicable to any parent. Before the first week of the class, we were asked to write down our goal in parenting. In the first class, one parent shared her well-meaning parental goal, that her child would be able to bounce back from adversity.

Being able to bounce back from adversity is a good thing, but the people in the group were believers who had adopted or were in the process of adopting. We wondered how there could be parenting goals in this class that were void of God and His desires for parents. But by God's grace, the class helped every parent, including us, to deepen their understanding of God's desires in parenting and how to get there. I believe we find the purest picture of what God desires in the story of Samson. In Judges 13, an angel comes to a woman who was barren and tells her that she will have a child that has a purpose from God. She tells her husband, and he does what we all would do—asks God to send the angel to him so he knows what to do.

Then Manoah prayed to the Lord and said, "O Lord, please let the man of God whom you sent come again to us and teach us what we are to do with the child who will be born." And God listened to the voice of Manoah, and the angel of God came again to the woman as she sat in the field. But

Manoah her husband was not with her. So the woman ran quickly and told her husband, "Behold, the man who came to me the other day has appeared to me." And Manoah arose and went after his wife and came to the man and said to him, "Are you the man who spoke to this woman?" And he said, "I am." And Manoah said, "Now when your words come true, what is to be the child's manner of life, and what is his mission?" And the angel of the LORD said to Manoah, "Of all that I said to the woman let her be careful. She may not eat of anything that comes from the vine, neither let her drink wine or strong drink, or eat any unclean thing. All that I commanded her let her observe" (Judges 13:8–14).

What we find here is that the angel from God doesn't lay out a step-by-step plan from birth but rather the call to observe all he commanded her to observe. In essence, he tells the parents to be faithful to the Lord's commands. Too often as parents, we forget that our faithfulness to God is vital to our role as parents. If you remember the story, Samson's story wasn't really a picture of obedience. In fact, he is more a picture of pride gone awry leading to an early death. Do you think his parents failed as parents? To be honest, much like us, Samson made his own poor decisions despite what he was taught. The crazy thing is that the next time we hear of Samson is in Hebrews 11, the so-called hall of fame for the faithful. How can that be? Because in the end, he fulfilled the purposes of God. He judged Israel for 20 years and ended up humble before the Lord.

Do you think Samson's parents were ultimately proud that God considered Samson faithful despite his series of poor choices? I'm sure they were. You see, even a perfect father has children that make poor choices despite what they are taught and how it was taught (see Gen. 3). But parents need to keep in mind that God's purposes are sometimes unknown, so we can't let visible results drive the measurement of our successful parenting. What we have to do is focus on being faithful to God in every role we have—father, mother, husband, wife, vocation counselor, volunteer, servant. In other words, to be a good parent, we should strive to be better servants of Christ.

One of our problems is that many of us have hurts that have not been healed, and we are carrying those wounds into our parenting lens. We don't see God correctly and don't understand how He sees us, either. This poor theology of God and His redeemed enters our daily interaction with our kids, and we sometimes feel hopeless. The truth is that God knows our hearts, our children's hearts, and His purposes, so we must maintain hope that He has it all under control. According to Acts 17, He divinely chose to match us not only with our children but also with the parents who might have been an active part of our hurts as well.

So what do we do? Should we just count on God to work it all out? Not at all! Instead, we actively war against our flesh, seek out healing for our hurts, and strive to point our children to the perfect Father. We do this by being intentional in as many areas as we can. Being intentional is a lost art in parenting. It is easy to forget that children are learning all the time, not just during designed teaching times. But being intentional isn't just what we do. We must explain why we are doing the things we do. For instance, placing a child in time-out because he or she disobeyed could be seen as punishment to a child. It is completely different to speak to the child about your love that sent him or her to the time-out. Children must know that God doesn't punish His children but gives discipline to train His children. The time-out was not meant to punish but to discipline. Their actions reveal they believe the lie that their way is better than God's (Rom. 1). You desire to be with them, but sin separates us from God, and the time-out was a picture of that separation. God sent His Son to end that separation for those who repent and believe. If children repent of their disobedience, their time-out ends, and we ask God for forgiveness together.

This type of intentionality can be tiresome, but after all, doesn't faithfulness require us to speak of God's ways from morning until night (Deut. 6:4–7)? Sure, we wish there was a step-by-step guide for every situation we face, but in end, all of us come to a place where we are clueless about how to be faithful in a particular situation. We must always remember that being faithful is not measured in an instant but over time. We are being transformed into the image of His Son more and more. The more we are like Jesus, the more we image the Father. The more we image the Father, the more faithful we are as parents. Oh, to be like Him!

God is slow to anger and abounding in steadfast love. Our heavenly Father never disciplines us with a scowl on His face, and neither should we scowl at our children. Yes, we should catechize our children and do daily devotionals, but it will be our daily parenting that will teach what we actually believe about God more than anything. Let us desire to be faithful, leave the results to Him, and trust that even our best parenting moments won't be enough to save their souls. Their salvation is not by our works but by His grace alone.

May grace abound in our homes!

Additional Resources for Your Home

• •

There are many great resources we could recommend, but these should give you a good starting point.

For Parents

Family Shepherds: Calling and Equipping Men to Lead Their Homes – Voddie Baucham Jr.
Directed solely to a father, this book is explained well in the title.

Family Driven Faith: Doing What It Takes to Raise Sons and Daughters Who Walk with God –
    Voddie Baucham Jr.
A challenging read that calls parents to get into the game and raise their children as God
    calls them. Toward the end, the book does push some family and church integration.
    The vast majority of the book is very insightful.

Shepherding a Child's Heart – Tedd Tripp
This book comes back to the gospel and the true nature of our children's hearts and how
    God graciously provides a solution in the scriptures.

This Momentary Marriage: A Parable of Permanence – John Piper
This is a fabulous book that properly roots marriage within the context of God's plans and pur-
    poses. It is a must-read for any parent wanting to display the gospel daily to their children.

Treasuring God in Our Traditions – Noël Piper
Gives parents a needed reminder that what we pass along to our children is very important.

The Connected Child: Bring Hope and Healing to Your Adoptive Family — Karyn B. Purvis, Ph.D.,
   David R. Cross, Ph.D., and Wendy Lyons Sunshine
Written for adoptive parents, this book is a must-read for any parent looking to parent
   with the goal of reaching a child's heart.

For the Family

Bibles

The Jesus Story Book Bible: Every Story Whispers His Name — Sally Lloyd-Jones
This book works its way through the Bible showing how everything points to Jesus. Great
   for pre-school age and early elementary.

The Gospel Story Bible: Discovering Jesus in the Old and New Testaments — Marty Machowski
A wide range of stories from both the Old and New Testaments. Provides questions after
   each story to foster teaching. Good for school age kids, especially those who read
   on their own.

Long Story Short: Ten-Minute Devotions to Draw Your Family to God — Marty Machowski
Easy 10-minute devotionals that any parent can do.

Books

The Big Book of Questions & Answers about Jesus — Ferguson Sinclair
A great resource for any family when it comes to answering questions and doing devotionals.

Big Truths for Young Hearts: Teaching and Learning the Greatness of God — Bruce A. Ware
Systematically gives parents chapters to read and helps them teach theology to their
   children.

Conclusion

Halfway Herbert – Francis Chan
A great little kid's book that introduces kids to the fact that they need Jesus and the
   Spirit to give them a whole heart.

The Big Red Tractor and the Little Village – Francis Chan
This kid's book masterfully teaches kids the power of the Holy Spirit available to us.

Ronnie Wilson's Gift – Francis Chan
A touching kid's story that shows what it looks like to serve Christ while here on earth.

Jesus is Coming Back! – Debby Anderson
A fun book for toddlers that teaches them that Jesus will return.

Little Pilgrim's Progress: From John Bunyan's Classic – Helen L. Taylor
An absolutely great read for young readers but even better if read by a parent. Read a
   chapter or two a night after dinner or use it as a devotional by asking questions after
   each chapter.

God Knows My Name – Debby Anderson
Another fun book for toddlers that teaches them about God.

A Forever Home for Antonio: A Gospel Adoption Journey – Chris Chavez
A gospel-centered kids book on adoption. A great story to help parents build a framework
   to explain adoption.

The Gospel Advent Book – Chris Chavez
A 25-day family devotional written to help parents teach about the coming of the Messiah.

Golly's Folly: The Prince Who Wanted It All – Eleazar Ruiz and Rebekah Ruiz
www.gollysfolly.com

Conclusion

Incredibly illustrated book based on the book of Ecclesiastes. There is also a workbook available.

Music

Seeds Family Worship
- www.seedsfamilyworship.com
- Fun, scripture-based songs on CD that can help your family sing and worship together
- Can be found on iTunes as well

Jesus Came to Save Sinners
- Download for free at www.thevillagechurch.net/resources/music/
- Fun and teaches theology of the gospel and God's character
- Can be found on iTunes as well

Bethel Music Kids
- www.bethelmusic.com/albums/come-alive/
- Fun and engaging kid versions of their music
- Can be found on iTunes as well

Crazy Praise CDs
- Can be found on iTunes

Conclusion

Acknowledgments

· · · · · · · · · · · · · · · · · · · ·

Luke Damoff – Your theological pushback and encouragement helped me produce a much more loving resource for parents. Your thoughts challenged me and actually helped me understand my own marriage in a deeper way. We didn't have to agree on everything, but we did have to be honest in our thoughts, and you did that with grace. Thank you for your obedience to what the Bible says and not what I wanted it to say.

John Blase – I am immensely blessed to have the Lord deliver an editor of your caliber to my doorstep. You were able to help me convey thoughts with much needed clarity. Any reader who finds any flaws with the writing must understand that you were working with an untrained writer, and you are to be commended for your work. You are a blessing, and I am thankful you accepted this project.

Mike Brown – Who would have guessed that two fraternity knuckleheads would one day collaborate on a Bible-teaching resource for parents? Your gifting has always been evident, and I pray that many children are inspired by your wonderful artwork. I am so glad to have taken on this project with a friend and brother in the Lord.

Antonio Chavez Jr. – Dad, I'll never know how life would have been if you had not been killed in an accident when I was 6. Who you were when you were alive remains a mystery to me in so many ways. By all accounts, you were the man I hope to be one day. But know this, your absence has been a driver in my family.

Conclusion

It wasn't until age 39 that I grieved your being gone, wondering if we would have been friends if we met that day. That weekend filled with tears is a marker in my life, and as much as I wish you had been there when I was growing up, I can now thank God for your early death. I now have a heart to be a father that I might not have had, and this book is rooted in that heart. Whatever DNA I have that reflects God's goodness, I thank you for it and hope to be your friend when Jesus returns.

Our Kickstarter Contributors – A special thank you to all listed here and the many others who gave to help bring this project to life.

Joe and Lindsay Rodden

The Clarke Family

The Shanks Family

The Rozelle Family

Jinohn Renea

Ben and Gina Killmer

The Embry Family

The Berend Family

The Barba Family

The Rabalais Family

The Bowman Family

The Hull Family

The Ullmann Family

The Pierce Family

The White Family

The Ayers Family

The Miller Family

Rich and Staci Cass

The Michaelis Family

The Schroyer Family

The Lee Family

Cass Family Charitable Trust

The Juergens Family

The Jung Family

Conclusion

About the Illustrator

Michael Brown is an award-winning actor/director of theatre and film, as well as an author/illustrator. Michael has had a cartoon syndicated by King Features and a feature film distributed by Lionsgate. He enjoys the unique challenges each artistic medium brings. Michael lives in Texas with his beautiful wife, Cheree, and his children: Abby, Luke, Lydia, and Phoebe. He never has to look far from the cast of characters living in his house to find fresh artistic inspiration. Visit Michael online at www.browncowproductions.com.

CPSIA information can be obtained
at www.ICGtesting.com
Printed in the USA
BVHW052111190319
543158BV00003B/4/P